To Guy  muse.
a friend,

Thank you, Guy, for your assistance in editing this book and for your encouragement to write this revised edition.

You & Linda are special friends and I am blessed that you are now a part of this deliverance ministry and a part of Spiritual Freedom Network.

Love in Christ,
Dr James E Tent

BREAKING CHAINS OF DARKNESS

AND

SETTING THE CAPTIVES FREE

Revised Edition
October 2016

A special thank you to Dr. Tim DeTroye for the hours he spent assisting with the formatting of this book. Also, a note of gratitude to Guy Caple for the time he spent editing. Without their efforts this book may still be in my computer or stored in a cloud.

ISBN   978-1-365-38703-6

Printed in the United States

Sabaoth Ministries
2016

All Bible references are from the New King James version unless otherwise stated.

Proceeds from this book will be used to expand God's Kingdom through Sabaoth Ministries and Spiritual Freedom Network. Both ministries are dedicated to setting God's people free from demonic strongholds.

PREFACE

When we accept Christ as our Savior, we become sons of God, washed clean by His blood, and when we die we go to heaven. This, however, does not mean we are totally free and our problems will come to an end. We are still bound by our past: struggling with hurt, bitterness, unforgiveness, depression, illness, addiction, or just plain feeling defeated in life, to mention a few.

Why are we still in bondage to situations from our past? It is because our spirit is born again, but our soul (will, emotions and mind) and our physical bodies need to be renewed and transformed. It is these areas that may need deliverance.

The following pages include a comprehensive biblically based study about the ministry of deliverance and spiritual warfare as established by Jesus Christ. It includes a wide variety of topics directly connected to this most awesome ministry; such as: the origin of Satan and demons, can a Christian have a demon, the work and activity of demonic spirits, generational curses, sole ties, spiritual warfare, the believer's authority, ministry to children, the deliverance process and much more.

This first edition of this manual was written during the preparation of a course initially offered in Aiken, South Carolina. Since that time it has been used as a supplement in several classes and training sessions in South Carolina, Alabama, Tennessee, Texas, Mexico and Michigan.

The purposes for the development of this manual are to (1) educate the Body of Christ regarding the ministry of deliverance and spiritual warfare; and to (2) train those who desire to be used of God to set their brethren free from the torment of demonic spirits.

This manual can be used for personal or group study, or as a teaching guide for teaching this as a course or Bible study.

CONTENT

As a farmer once told me: "I milk a lot of cows, but I churn my own butter." This is a good description of how this manual was developed. The material presented here was derived from our personal study of the Scriptures and our experience of more than twenty-seven years in the deliverance ministry. Our knowledge has also been enhanced by the following individuals: Frank and Ida Hammond; Dr. Henry Malone; Rick Renner; G. Maldonado, and John Eckhardt.

The original intent for developing this manual was to teach a comprehensive course on deliverance and spiritual warfare rather than for wide spread distribution. However, it has gained increased popularity throughout the Body of Christ since it first printing. Therefore, it has been recommended that we write this revised edition providing additional and updated information.

PREPARATION

There is a book written by Jack Handey called "Fuzzy Memories." In this book he tells a story about a bully who would demand his lunch every day. Since he was a smaller boy he would always give it to him. Then one day he decided to fight back, so he started taking karate lessons, but the instructor wanted $5.00 a lesson. That was too much money so he decided it was cheaper to pay the bully, so he gave up karate.

Too many Christians believe it is easier to pay the bully than learn how to defeat the enemy themselves. They fail to realize they are living on a battlefield and not a playground. Every Christian is in a battle with the enemy and must become prepared to defeat his foe. The pages of this manual are your karate lessons - the major weapon God has given His church to defeat Satan and his evil spirits.

TABLE OF CONTENTS

PREFACE 3
CONTENT 4
PREPARATION 5
TABLE OF CONTENTS 6
PERSONAL EXPERIENCE 14
INTRODUCTION 16
    What is Deliverance? 18
    Why is Deliverance Such a Mystery? 20
    Deliverance vs. Inner Healing 20
    The Church and Demons 21
    Why You Need to Understand Deliverance 22

CHAPTER ONE 24
    DELIVERANCE IS THE CHILDREN'S BREAD 24
        The Ministry of Deliverance 25
        The Solution to Flesh 27
        The Solution to Demons 27

CHAPTER TWO 28
    OUR IDENTITY IN CHRIST 28
        You are loved by God the Father 29
        You were purchased at a steep price 29
        We are entitled to a clean conscience 30
        Your sins are no longer a part of you 31
        We have peace with God 31
        We are clothed with the righteousness of Jesus 32
        You are seated with Christ-a position of authority 33
        Some of topics we will discuss later on are: 35

CHAPTER THREE 36
    THE ORIGIN OF SATAN AND DEMONS 36
        Satan: 36
        Descriptions Of Demons 37
        Characteristics of Demons 37
        Capabilities of Demons 38
        How Jesus Dealt With Demons? 38

CHAPTER FOUR 39
    CAN A CHRISTIAN HAVE A DEMON 39

A Final Word About Christians and Demons..*41*

CHAPTER FIVE **42**

SHOULD A NON-CHRISTIAN RECEIVE DELIVERANCE?............................42

CHAPTER SIX **43**

HOW CAN DEMONS GAIN ACCESS?..43

CHAPTER SEVEN **51**

SATAN'S ATTACKS BY INTRUSION 51
- *Strategy 1:* *52*
- *Strategy 2* *53*
- *Strategy 3* *54*
- *Strategy 4* *54*
- *Strategy 5* *55*

CHAPTER EIGHT...**56**

TIHE WORK AND ACTIVITY 56
OF DEMONIC SPIRITS 56
- *Physical Infirmities*..*56*
- *Spiritual Oppression or Delusion* *57*
- *MOST COMMON SYMPTOMS OF INDWELLING SPIRITS* *58*

CHAPTER NINE **60**

THE CHURCH UNDER ATTACK 60
- *Common Demons that Attack the Church* *61*
- *The Spirit of Jezebel* *62*
- *First let me tell you about the man who married Jezebel.* *62*
- *The Human Being:* *63*
- *The Church*..*63*
- *The Nation:*..*63*
- *What Are The Characteristics of a Person Under The Influence of Jezebel?*....*64*
- *A Pharisaic Spirit*..*64*
- *How do you know when this spirit is in operation* *64*
- *The Spirit of Witchcraft* *64*

CHAPTER TEN **66**

SIGNS OF DEMONIC HARASSMENT 66
AND OPPRESSION 66
- *The person fasts and prays without results* *66*
- *The person feels harassed* *66*

CHAPTER ELEVEN **67**

SIGNS OF DEMONIC INFESTATION 67
   The person feels tormented..67
   Areas Affected By Demon Spirits 69

CHAPTER TWELVE 71

GENERATIONAL CURSES 71
   Examples in the Bible of Iniquity Passed Through the Generations:................77
   The First Murder 77
   What Was King David Thinking? 77
   And Then There Was The Curse of Canaan 78
   How About Those Ungodly Amorites?..78
   THE PROCESS FOR BREAKING CURSES 81
   AFTER BREAKING THESE CURSES 81

CHAPTER THIRTEEN 82

THE CAUSES OF GENERATIONAL CURSES 82
   The Occult..82
   All Forms of Illicit or Unnatural Sex 82
   Not Honoring or Respecting Parents 83
   To Curse That Which God Has Blessed 83
   To Steal That Which Belongs to God 83
   Injustices 84

CHAPTER FOURTEEN 85

SIGNS AND INDICATIONS 85
OF GENERATIONAL CURSES 85
   Mental and Emotional Disturbances 85
   Infertility..85
   Disintegration of the Family 86
   Poverty or Continual Economic Insufficiency...86
   Self-Imposed Curses..86

CHAPTER FIFTEEN 87

THE BELIEVERS AUTHORITY...87
   The Meat of our Authority..89
   Authority to Minister to Others 91
   Lead People to Christ...92
   Baptize Them in the Holy Spirit..92
   Minister to the Brokenhearted 92
   A major part of Jesus' ministry was casting out demons...............................92
   As a believer you also have the authority to cast evil spirits out of the brethren. This is simply doing what Jesus did and told us to do. 92
   Heal The Sick..93

Breaking Bondages *93*
Specific examples of bondages would include: *93*
Blessings and Impartations *93*

CHAPTER SIXTEEN **94**
OUR SPIRITUAL ENEMY 94
1. Our battle is against PRINCIPALITIES. *95*
2. Our warfare is against POWERS *96*
3. We wrestle against THE RULERS OF DARKNESS OF *98*
THIS WORLD. *98*
4. We wrestle against SPIRITUAL WICKEDNESS IN HIGH *99*
PLACES *99*

CHAPTER SEVENTEEN **101**
SPIRITUAL WARFARE 101
So How Are We to Prepare For Spiritual Battle? *102*
Let me repeat: *106*
SAMPLE WARFARE PRAYER *111*

CHAPTER EIGHTEEN **114**
LEGAL RIGHTS AND RECLAIMING 114
LEGAL GROUND 114
What is a Legal Right? *114*

CHAPTER NINETEEN **117**
SOUL TIES 117
Demonic Soul Ties *118*
Ties Formed Through Fornication *118*
Ties With Evil Companions *119*
Perverted Family Ties *120*
Soul Ties With The Dead *121*
Demonic Soul Ties Within The Church *122*
Influence of Like Spirits *122*
The Power of Soul Ties *123*
Fellowship *124*
Breaking Demonic Soul Ties *125*
Command the evil spirits associated with the soul ties to leave you in the Name of Jesus Christ, the Son of God. *126*

CHAPTER TWENTY **127**
UNGODLY BELIEF SYSTEMS 127
What Are Ungodly Belief Systems? *127*
Where Do Ungodly Beliefs Come From? *129*

- *Conclusion* 132
- *A Suggested Prayer for Replacing* 132
- *Ungodly Belief Systems* 132

CHAPTER TWENTY-ONE 133

DEMONIC STRONGHOLDS 133
- *What is a Stronghold?* 133
- *Two Very Important Strongholds* 133
- *How to tear down a stronghold* 134

CHAPTER TWENTY-TWO 135

THE DELIVERANCE MINISTRY AND CHILDREN 135
- *Key Truths In Deliverance For Children* 136
- *When The Womb Is Unsafe* 137
- DIFFERENCES BETWEEN THE DELIVERANE OF AN ADULT AND A CHILD 139
- *Maintaining Deliverance* 141
- *Final Action* 143

CHAPTER TWENTY-THREE 144

NECESSARY STEPS TO DELIVERANCE 144
- *Repentance* 145

CHAPTER TWENTY-FOUR 147

THE DELIVERANCE TEAM 147
- *Size and Composition* 147
- *Team Unity* 148
- *Functions of Team Members* 148

CHAPTER TWENTY-FIVE 149

OBSTACLES TO DELIVERANCE 149
- OBSTACLES AND UNTRUTHS 150
- Fear At The Mention of Demons, The Devil And Deliverance. 150
- Deliverance is Valid; However, It Should Be Left To Experts 151
- Christians Cannot Have Demons 151
- Demons Have No Activity In Civilized Countries. They Are Active Only In Remote Countries Where Witchcraft and Idolatry Prevail. 152
- They Will Come Back Seven Times Worse 152
- Deliverance Must Never Be Done In Public 153
- Jesus Did It All For Us. We Don't Have To Fight 154

CHAPTER TWENTY-SIX 155

DELIVERANCE FROM SELF 155

CHAPTER TWENTY-SEVEN 162

SPIRITUAL HOUSECLEANING 162
- Symptoms of a House that is Spiritually Contaminated 162
- Items That Need to be Removed and Destroyed 163

CHAPTER TWENTY-EIGHT 165

DEMON GROUPINGS 165
- DELIVERANCE GROUPINGS 168

CHAPTER TWENTY-NINE 172

SPIRIT OF REJECTION 172

CHAPTER THIRTY 176

THE LACK OF FORGIVNESS 176
- Forgiveness is Not an Option but a Command from the Lord 176
- Lack of Forgiveness is a Bait for the Enemy 177
- The Consequences of Not Forgiving 177

CHAPTER THIRTY-ONE 179

THE ROOT OF BITTERNESS 179
- What Causes Bitterness? 180
- When someone or something is taken from you. 180
- When someone hurts you. 181
- What Are The Signs of the Root of Bitterness? 181
- Consequences of the Root of Bitterness 181

CHAPTER THIRTY-TWO 183

SPIRIT OF GUILT 183
- Characteristics of a Person with a Sense of Guilt 183
- Self-punishment 184
- Unworthiness 184
- Compulsive behaviors 184
- False humility 185
- The Consequences of Guilt 185

CHAPTER THIRTY-THREE 187

SIGNS OF THE ZODIAC 187

CHAPTER THIRTY-FOUR 189

POLTERGEIST 189
- How does one evict poltergeist spirits? 190

CHAPTER THIRTY-FIVE 192

DEMONS CLASSIFIED BY MONTH	192
CHAPTER THIRTY-SIX	**195**
THE CURSE OF ILLEGITIMACY	195
Prayer to Break the Curse of Illegitimacy	*198*
CHAPTER THIRTY-SEVEN	**199**
THE UNUSUAL AND BIZARRE	199
CHAPTER THIRTY-EIGHT	**207**
INCUBUS AND SUCCUBUS	207
CHAPTER THIRTY-NINE	**209**
DEMONIC MANIFESTATIONS	209
CHAPTER FORTY	**212**
SHOULD I BE A DELIVERÆNCE MINISTER?	212
CHAPTER FORTY-ONE	**219**
POTENTIAL PITFALLS	219
Those In Ministry	*219*
Those Receiving Deliverance	*220*
CHAPTER FORTY-TWO	**222**
THE DELIVERANCE PROCESS	222
PRE-QUALIFY YOUR CANDIDATE	*222*
PRE-DELIVERANCE	*224*
THE DELIVERANCE	*227*
How To Cast Out Demons	*229*
CHAPTER FORTY-THREE	**231**
MAINTAINING YOUR DELIVERANCE	231
Things You Must Know to Maintain Your Deliverance	*232*
Examine and Change Your Activities	*233*
By Faith Accept God's Word as True	*236*
Rejection:	*237*
Anxiety & Worry	*237*
Bitterness, Unforgiveness, Anger	*238*
Control, Manipulation, Intimidation, Pride	*239*
Fears	*240*
Shame, Guilt and Condemnation	*240*
Sexual Immorality and Covetousness	*241*
Infirmities (Sickness & Disease)	*242*

- *Violence* *242*
- *Murder* *243*
- *Rebellion* *244*
- *Abandonment* *244*

APPENDIX ONE 246

TYPES OF OCCULTISM 246
- *Other Areas of Occultism* *249*

APPENDIX TWO 250

DELIVERANCES PRAYERS AND CONFESSIONS 250
- *Opening Prayer* *250*
- *General Confession and Prayer* *251*
- *Forgiveness Prayer* *251*
- *Occult Confession Prayer* *251*
- *Loosing From Witchcraft & Related Powers* *252*
- *Loosing From Domination Prayer* *252*
- *Breaking Curses Confession* *252*
- *Breaking Soul Ties* *252*

APPENDIX THREE 254

THE FULL ARMOR OF GOD 254
- *Commentary* *254*
- PIECES OF ARMOR 256
- BELT OF TRUTH 256
- BREASTPLATE OF RIGHTEOUSNESS 256
- SHIELD OF FAITH 258
- SWORD OF THE SPIRIT 259

PERSONAL EXPERIENCE

(That Which Initiated our Involvement in Deliverance)

My wife and I grew up in non-Pentecostal churches and had never heard about deliverance. Even after we became spirit-filled, tongue talking, water walking Pentecostals, we had not heard deliverance preached or taught.

We had recently moved to a new area of Michigan and began attending a satellite church of a much larger church located in Indiana.

During that time I was suffering from severe depression. No medication, even in unprecedented doses, was effective. The symptoms became so severe I was strongly contemplating suicide and was probably within days of ending my life.

Medically it was referred to as "clinical depression" caused by a chemical imbalance in the brain. I was about to discover that my depression was demonic; specifically a generational curse that came down the bloodline from my mother and grandmother and who knows how long before that. My children were also the recipients of this awful illness (curse) but were being successfully treated with medication.

One day a man who also attended the same satellite church we attended stopped in to see me at work, and I expressed my need for help as I could no longer live, or even function, under my current circumstances. This meeting was a divine appointment of God as he began to explain how God often heals through the ministry of deliverance. As he spoke about healing and deliverance it was as if I had been in a dark room and God suddenly opened all the doors and windows and the light of truth filled the room.

Two days later this same man of God walked into my place of business and said; "Jim, today is the day God is going to set you free." These are words I will never forget as they changed my life forever. That night they broke the generational curse; I went through deliverance and when the demonic spirit of depression left I felt it leave and I shouted; "it's gone." At that very instant, both my children who were present also shouted; "it's gone."

God had delivered and healed each of us that night in August, 1989. That same night God delivered me from my addiction to nicotine and healed me of lip cancer, which I had developed from smoking a pipe for many years.

That was the beginning of an incredible journey that has lasted nearly 27 years.

INTRODUCTION

Every reputable Bible scholar agrees that we have an adversary who hates the gospel, hates the presence of the church, works around the clock to discredit the message of Jesus Christ, and has a systematic plan to attack every believer.

In chapter six we are going to discuss specifically how demons enter into a person's life. However, generally but not inclusively, it can be said that they primarily enter into a believer's life through the believer's negligence. He slips through an uncommitted, un-renewed area of the mind ....a loophole--- and then begins to wage warfare against the mind and flesh of that individual.

Regardless of the how they enter, too many Christians today hide from this foe, thinking that if they ignore him, he will ignore them. WRONG!

Far too many in the body of Christ have believed and/or have been misinformed that when we accept Jesus as Lord and Savior we are freed from demonic influences. This is a grievous error and the reason so many Christians suffer needlessly. We must understand that in the spiritual realm you only lose when you quit. Satan has the power to overpower us, but he does not the authority to do so.

When we accept Jesus Christ as our Savior we become a new creation, our sins are washed away by the shed blood of Christ, and we become children of God. But we are not totally free nor do our problems just automatically end. We still struggle with such things as sickness & disease, hurts, emotional or psychological problems, rejection, anger, bitterness, and many other problems.

As believers we are still in bondage to our past. Our spirit has been born again, but our body and soul still needs to be renewed and transformed. Our soul is our will, our mind and our emotions and our body is the physical element of our being.

The solution to these areas of torment in our lives is the ministry of deliverance. A ministry introduced by Jesus and one which He has commanded us to ministry to one another (Mark 16:17-18).

The bottom line is this: Demon spirits can invade and indwell human bodies. It is their objective to do so. They are unnecessary and undesirable trespassers whom we can evict.

UNDERSTANDING DELIVERANCE

What is Deliverance?
Deliverance is the ministry Jesus introduced as He healed the sick and set free those tormented by demons (also referred to as unclean or demonic spirits). Deliverance is the process of expelling demons. Scripture specifically refers to deliverance as "casting out demons."

However, it is more than that: Deliverance is one aspect of the total salvation that Jesus purchased on the cross. Salvation is more than a ticket to heaven. Salvation includes God's **TOTAL** provision for human need, including our pain and suffering.

The Greek word saved is a form of the Greek word *sozo*. This Greek word is not only translated as saved (salvation) but it is also translated with words like **healed, made whole, delivered or set free.** When Jesus cast out a demon he occasionally said; "Your faith has set you free (sozo)" or "Your faith has healed (sozo) you."

Therefore, salvation is not just escaping hell but it includes healing and deliverance from evil spirits.

Deliverance is what Jesus did and what He told us to do in Mark 16:16; that we are told to "cast out demons." In fact, it is the first sign that Jesus told us would follow His believers: "In My name they will cast out demons. .." (Mark 16:17). Therefore, deliverance is a command.

The term deliverance is used to encompass both the process and the result of one's liberation from demonic bondage. Deliverance is achieved, as we said, by driving out evil spirits using your authority in the name of Jesus. Because Jesus said we would cast out demons in "His Name."

The Value of Deliverance
Deliverance (the process of expelling demons) is not a panacea or a cure all. Yet it is an important part of what God is doing in His church.

Those in the deliverance ministry do not have to go out and look for prospects. It is evident when God places a desire for purity in the hearts of His people. It is not necessary to encourage anyone to receive from this ministry, let them request it of you. Because, you need to know they are serious and committed.

It becomes obvious when a believer wants to continue in their spiritual growth and realize that every hindrance to their spiritual growth must be eliminated.

God is coming for a bride that is spotless and without wrinkle. The church is to become "holy and without blemish" therefore, unclean spirits must be purged from our lives.

Demons are enemies to both the gifts and the fruits of the Spirit. They keep them from manifesting in a believer's life.

Example: Prophecy. The scripture says; "...Let us prophecy in proportion to our faith" (Rom. 12:6). The demon of doubt and/or unbelief can block the flow of prophecy.

Example: Love. The fruit of love is a special target of Satan. Love is something we are to receive as well as give. The demon of resentment can defeat love in a person's life.

Many people cannot understand why they are unable to love others as they ought. Such a problem is a strong indication of the presence of resentment or unforgiveness. Resentment usually invites in other demons like bitterness, hatred and anger.

The spirit of rejection will also hinder your ability to love. This is a very common spirit and is often a "strong or ruling" spirit within an individual.

One important thing to remember is that needing deliverance is not just about what you did, but what the enemy has done to you. The need for deliverance is not something that should make you feel guilty but rather you should view it as an opportunity for freedom. Not only does deliverance bring emotional and spiritual healing, and the freedom from tormenting spirits like rejection, bitterness and anger, but it is often necessary for physical healing as was seen in Jesus' ministry. When we pray for someone and they are not healed, it is possible that they need deliverance from a demonic spirit that is causing the illness. When the spirit is gone then you can pray for the healing.

Why is Deliverance Such a Mystery?

The Bible is full of mysteries, but the mystery of deliverance is seldom taught, and I believe it is one mystery most people have difficulty understanding. Deliverance is seldom ever mentioned in our churches today; I believe this is true because few pastors and church leaders themselves understand this ministry and/or they have been misinformed as to its validity for today.

The modern day church attendee has also not been taught about the need for spiritual warfare in their daily life and therefore, they have a tendency to ignore the enemy instead of facing him head on. By doing so they become an easier target for Satan and his demons.

It is also true that the mind set of most Christians is they either think others may have demons but surely they do not; or they question the idea that a Christian could actually have a demon. Because of this mindset, we have pastors, church leaders and members of our congregation's that form an opposition to the deliverance ministry. The problem with such a mindset is that they not only miss out on this awesome ministry and remain bound, but opposition to deliverance fits into the category of doubt, skepticism and ridicule of divine things and is actually an open door for an attack from Satan and his demons (see Chapters Four & Six).

As you continue this study you will realize that the ministry of deliverance is not a complicated or frightening ministry. Rather it is a ministry initiated and set in the church by Jesus Himself to "set the captives free" from demonic spirits that negatively influence their lives.

Deliverance vs. Inner Healing

Some people refer to deliverance as inner healing while others separate the two. Those who separate the two usually refer to inner healing as the result of one's deliverance from demons affecting our emotions and/or psychological aspects of our lives. Therefore, inner healing is when a person is delivered and thereby delivered from past traumatic and painful experiences caused by others. The use of the term deliverance by those that separate deliverance and inner healing refers to deliverance as being set free from demons affecting our physical body.

Based upon the past twenty seven years of experience in this ministry, I would suggest that they are somewhat interchangeable. In other words, I would suggest that inner healing is simply the result of deliverance; the result of casting out demons whether the healing benefit is emotional, psychological or physical. Regardless of whether one calls it inner healing or deliverance the result is the same: people are set free and healed when demons are cast out of them.

The Church and Demons

Christians throughout the United States are currently praying for a great end-time revival. The Christian church is ripe for revival and it appears that God is about to pour out His Spirit. But He may be waiting because many in the Body of Christ are not yet ready. Let me explain:

First, when revival comes, Satan will attack both Christians and churches by increasing his demonic attacks. If the Body of Christ is not ready for such attacks, revival will be short lived. We must understand and begin to utilize the weapons God has provided (spiritual warfare, deliverance, understanding and breaking generational curses, knowing our authority as a believer, etc.). One of the main characteristics of any revival lasting longer than six months to one year is the early establishment of deliverance ministries. Argentina may be our best example. They developed an aggressive deliverance ministry in a large variety of denominations and have maintained a revival that has lasted more than fifteen years.

The city of Almolonga in Guatemala, a city of 18,000 people, is another great example of a long term revival based upon an aggressive deliverance ministry. Twenty-five years ago this city was filled with poverty, lack of moral restraint and a high percentage of alcoholics. Today 90% of the population are born-again Christians. They no longer have a need for a jail because crime no longer exists. The revival began because a pastor named Mariano Riscaje discovered he had the power, in Jesus name, to cast out demons. He started by delivering some 400 drunks in three months and revival has continued since that time.

Second, when revival comes, our churches will be inundated with new believers who are carrying a lot of baggage. That is, men and women with addictions, physical illness, emotional problems, past hurts and other tormenting demons. If our churches do not have deliverance ministries in place, how will these individuals be set free? How will churches be able to assist these new believers and make disciples as Jesus commanded us?

Prior to revival the body of Christ needs to be delivered themselves and become ready to participate in this ministry. Without it, revival will be short lived and many who come to Christ will again be lost. No one is exempt from demonic attacks or the indwelling of demonic spirits.

These demons may affect us to varying degrees but any demonic influence is a hindrance to spiritual growth and needs to be removed.

If the church is to prepare for a major move of God, it must accept, understand and utilize an aggressive deliverance ministry.

The current state of affairs in our nation is directly related to the condition of the church in our nation. If we are to improve the condition of our nation we must first improve the condition of our churches. This can only be done if we first improve ourselves individually. Individual revival can only be total and complete when we submit to deliverance and allow God to cleanse us and set us free from demonic bondage.

Why You Need to Understand Deliverance

Everyone has a personal need for deliverance. Granted, it is much more obvious with some than others. However, no one is exempt from what opens the door to demonic infestation in one's life; and we all are subject to generational curses. Once we study the ways Satan and his ungodly army operate, and how they enter individuals, you will gain an understanding of your possible need for deliverance.

You will discover that there are many areas in your life that you may think are a part of your personality but are in essence influenced by indwelling demonic spirits; or you may have hidden hurts from injustices done to you that you just try and bury. You may have difficultly forgiving; carrying feelings of guilt or condemnation over past sins; be depressed; feel insecure, inadequate or struggle with self-esteem. You may have an addiction to alcohol, drugs, nicotine, or pornography; be driven by lust; or feeling "just plan defeated" in life. Each of these situations can be demonic. On the other hand, many times serious and/or recurring illnesses are demonic in nature. Whatever the situation, deliverance is often the answer.

In addition, any of the aforementioned circumstances will also hinder your spiritual growth; and keep you from experiencing the fullness of God's blessings. As individuals are affected, so is the church as a whole. Thereby, they also miss the full outpouring of God's Spirit.

The church needs to prepare itself for an end-time revival by experiencing the benefits of deliverance and then learning how to administer this awesome gift of God. As I indicated in the introduction, the church will most likely be inundated with new believers who will bring with them a ton of baggage like addictions; physical and emotional illnesses; and numerous other tormenting spirits from which they will need deliverance. Without a good deliverance ministry, these poor souls have little chance of freedom.

Chapter One

DELIVERANCE IS THE CHILDREN'S BREAD

In Matthew 15:22-28 we read a story about a Canaanite who came to Jesus seeking deliverance for her daughter, who was being tormented by a demon. Because she was a Gentile (a non-believer) she was not included in God's covenant with the children of Israel, and not eligible to receive what she had asked.

She was definitely persistent and even used the words and covenant terms to which she was not entitled. She said, "Lord, Son of David, have mercy on me." When Jesus heard her speak, He did not respond right away. And after His disciples insisted that Jesus send her away, Jesus made two important statements. First He said; *"I was not sent except to the lost sheep of the house of Israel".* Jesus was referring to the people of Israel, those who believed and who were the only one's included in God's covenant. They were the only ones with legal rights to the blessings of the covenant, which included salvation, protection, provision, health and deliverance.

The second thing Jesus said was: *"It is not good to take the children's bread and throw it to the dogs."* The Jews referred to the Gentiles as "dogs". We can only conclude from this statement that deliverance is for the believer, the children of God.

This woman's desperate plea was fulfilled because of her demonstrated faith. But here is what happened. God's plan was for the gospel (repentance, salvation, healing, deliverance, etc.) to be presented to the people of the old covenant first. The call for the ingathering of Israel had to precede the ingathering of the Gentiles. This woman simply obtained a blessing that was for the future church.

After this, Jesus went to the cross and paid the price for all those who believed, both Jew and Gentile. Now anyone who believes in Him can enjoy salvation, healing, divine protection, deliverance and eternal life.

Deliverance belongs to all of us who are born again. Jesus paid the price for all our sins, rebellion, generational curses, rejection, and the list goes on and on.

You may ask: "If Jesus redeemed us from everything why is there a need for deliverance?" Let us not forget that the Spirit of God came to live in our spirit, but that our soul and body are still influenced by our past. For the Holy Spirit to live in fullness within us, we need to clean house.

There are many today, even in God's house, that have made a direct or indirect pact with the enemy through sin, doubt, skepticism and ridicule of divine things, occult activities, and improper attitudes. These individuals also carry generational curses in their bloodlines that must be broken and the corresponding demons removed.

<u>Many believers know they are free in theory, but fail to appropriate it</u>. That is, they fail to take hold of the complete freedom that belongs to them. God provided deliverance to set His people free from the bondage and torment of the devil and his demons.

The Ministry of Deliverance

Jesus Himself is the one who introduced deliverance. He actually began His ministry by casting out demons. Right after Jesus left the wilderness He called Peter, Andrew, James and John to follow Him. And immediately He went to Galilee, and what did He do there? He preached repentance, healed the sick and cast out demons.

Just like Jesus, when you cast out demons, it brings a direct confrontation with the kingdom of darkness. Satanic powers and the power of God confront one another; the result being deliverance from demonic infestation, along with all the oppression and torment.

In fact, scripture says that when you experience deliverance you have been visited by the kingdom of God. Specifically Matthew 12:28 says; *"But if I cast out demons by the spirit of God, surely the kingdom of God has come upon you."*

Then in verse 30 Jesus said; *"He who is not with Me is against Me, and he who does not gather with Me scatters abroad."* The church often uses this verse to evangelize, asking people if they are with Jesus or against Him. But that is not the context; Jesus is referring to the ministry of casting out demons.

There are Christians who believe in the ministries of preaching, teaching, healing and miracles, but when it comes to deliverance, they don't even like to discuss it. However, Jesus is saying in this text, if you are with Me to preach, teach and heal, you will be with Me in the ministry of deliverance.

I guarantee that if you can cast out demons; you will have no problem doing anything else for God.

The deliverance ministry exposes everything that is hidden in the heart of a person. God desires to bring more than salvation to those who believe.

Powerful demonic influences have been governing some families (as well as some cities, nations and even churches) for generations. But when the kingdom of God arrives, darkness must give way. Therefore, we can break generational curses over individuals and families and cast out demons. We also can weaken and eventually remove demonic spirits over specific territories through spiritual warfare.

Works of the Flesh vs. Demonic Infestation

There are some extreme beliefs in the church today. There are Christians who see demons everywhere and those that credit everything to manifestations of the flesh.

The flesh is our old Adamic nature, known as the old man or the carnal nature. It is the nature we inherited from Adam. Therefore, the problem of original sin is universal, and people from the fallen human race, inevitably come under the power of demons. If humanity had never sinned, we would not be vulnerable to demons.

The Solution to Flesh
The only remedy to conquer the flesh is *crucifixion.* Our old man has been crucified. The Apostle Paul said he had been crucified with Jesus Christ. Throughout the Bible we are taught what to do with the old nature, that is, to deny ourselves, take up the cross and follow Jesus each day.

"Knowing this, that the old man was crucified with Him, that the body of sin might be done away with, that we should no longer be slaves of sin." Romans 6:6

"I have been crucified with Christ; it is no longer I who live, but Christ lives in me; and the life which I now live in the flesh I live by faith in the Son of God, who loved me and gave Himself for me." Galatians 2:20

The Solution to Demons
Some believers have fasted, prayed, bound, rebuked, implored, and still have not gotten results. They have crucified the flesh but they still struggle with compulsive desires that affect their minds, bodies and emotions; all of which eventually lead to sin.

The only remedy for demons is to cast them out. Many believers have been taught that Christians cannot be possessed or even influenced by the devil, and that when they get born again, they become instantly set free. If this is true then why are many believers still dragging around bondages from the past that control and oppress them? Why are they hurt, tormented and even sick.

You cannot eliminate your desires and addictions by *trying* to crucify them. If they are caused by demons then they must be cast out.

Chapter Two

OUR IDENTITY IN CHRIST

This is an elementary subject that most Christians still do not fully understand, and it is a powerful key to spiritual breakthrough for countless believers around the globe today! Don't believe you're just an old forgiven sinner just because some pastor tells you so. Look these things up in the Word of God for yourself and know the truth. For Jesus said clearly that if we continue in His Word, we will know the truth and the truth will set us free!

John 8:32, *"And you shall know the truth, and the truth shall make you free."*

The opposite of truth is deception or false beliefs… and will cause you to live in bondage unnecessarily. This subject is no exception. If you fail to know who you are in Christ your chances of total freedom from demonic spirits is limited at best. Also, If you see yourself as a failure, you will not be able to boldly exercise your authority in Christ because you will feel unworthy (even after the Blood of Christ has made you worthy). If you claim to be unworthy after the Blood of Christ has made you worthy, then you are denying the work of Christ in your life!

Every believer needs to confess that, *"I am worthy, because JESUS' blood has made me worthy!*

Elements of Your Identity in Christ

You are loved by God the Father

You are loved by God, not because of what you've done, but because of who you are. The Bible tells us that while we were yet sinners, Christ died for us. He longed to have a relationship with you even before you became His child!

Romans 5:8, *"But God demonstrates His own love toward us, in that while we were still sinners Christ died for us."*

This one may be hard to get your mind around, but it is true. God loves us with the same love that He had towards Jesus Himself! Look at this passage in scripture:

John 17:23; *"I in them, and You in Me, that they may be made perfect in one, and that the world may know that You have sent Me, and have loved them, as You have loved Me."*

Jesus said that the greatest love a man can show for his friends, is when he lays down his life for them. Jesus laid down His life for us - that is how valuable and dear we are to Him!

John 15:13, *"Greater love has no one than this, than to lay down one's life for his friends."* As a matter of fact, if we don't realize the love of God, we cannot be filled with the fullness of God. We will lack His fullness in our lives until we come to know of His deep love for us:

Ephesians 3:17-19, *"That Christ may dwell in your hearts through faith; that you, being rooted and grounded in love, may be able to comprehend with all saints what is the width and length and depth and height; And to know the love of Christ, which passes knowledge; that you may be filled with all the fullness of God."*

You were purchased at a steep price

The wages of your sin is death (see Romans 6:23), but Jesus paid that price for you. God's Word tells us that we were purchased by the precious Blood of the Lamb:

I Corinthians 6:20, *"For you are bought with a price: therefore glorify God in your body, and in your spirit, which are God's."*

Revelations 5:9, *"And they sang a new song, saying: "You are worthy to take the book; and to open its seals; for You were slain, and have redeemed (meaning purchased) us to God by thy blood out of every tribe and tongue and people and nation."*

Why did Jesus purchase us with His own Blood? Because of His deep love for us, and He deeply desires to have a loving relationship with you and I.

We are justified and declared innocent

If you have repented of your sins and accepted the gift of God, referring to the forgiveness of sins through the precious shed Blood of Christ, then God's Word tells us that we are justified:

Galatians 2.16, *"Knowing that a man is not justified by the works of the law, but by the faith of Jesus Christ, even we have believed in Jesus Christ that we might be justified by the faith of Christ, and not by the works of the law; for by the works of the law shall no flesh be justified."*

The word *justified* in the above passage is derived from the Greek word *dikaioo*, which means, "to render (that is, show or regard as just or innocent". If a person is justified, it means they are made innocent or made just as if they have never sinned!

We are entitled to a clean conscience

Since our sins have been put away and removed from us, and we are justified, that is, made right with God, you and I are entitled to a clean and un-defiled conscience!

Hebrews 9:14, *"...how much more shall the blood of Christ, who through the eternal Spirit offered Himself without spot to God, purge your conscience from dead works to serve the living God".*

Dear Saint, if you are still beating yourself up over your past failures which have been nailed to the cross, you are denying the work that Christ has done for you! A clean conscience before the Lord agrees with what Christ has done in removing your sin and declaring you as justified or innocent before the Lord.

Your sins are no longer a part of you

The truth is that your sins have not simply been covered, but actually removed from your through the precious Blood of Christ, the removal of sins is a reality.

John 1.29, *"The next day John saw Jesus coming toward him, and said, "Behold The Lamb of God who takes away the sins of the world!"*

Matthew 26:28, *"For this is My blood of the new covenant, which is shed for many for the remission of sins."*

And if forgiving us wasn't enough, God Himself chose to FORGET our failures for His own sake. When He sees us, He doesn't want to remember our failures, He wants to see us as His precious child who stands blameless before Him:

Hebrews 10:17, *"...and their sins and their lawless deeds I will remember no more."*

We have peace with God

We have been justified and made right with God, therefore we have peace with God. This means that your relationship with God has been restored and you can boldly enter His presence with a clean conscience because of your faith in Christ Jesus and the work that He's done for us on the cross.
Romans 5:1, *"Therefore being justified by faith, we have peace with God through the Lord Jesus Christ."*

We are clothed with the righteousness of Jesus
As believers in Christ, there is a great exchange that has taken place. One of the things exchanged is our sin for Jesus' own righteousness. Let's take a look at a few scriptures:

Romans 3.22, *"Even the righteousness of God which is, through faith, in Jesus Christ to all and on all who believe.: for there is no difference."*

Romans 3:25, *"Whom God set forth to be a propitiation by His blood, through faith, to demonstrate His righteousness for the remission of sin that were previously committed"*

Romans 5:17, *"For by one man's offense death reigned through the one; much more those who receive abundance of grace and of the gift of righteousness will reign in life through the one, Jesus Christ."*

Jesus received what we deserved (punishment for our sins), and He gave us His righteousness in exchange!

You are made new in Christ — Born of God!
The old saying, "We are just forgiven sinners saved by grace" is so devastating because it actually denies the work that God has done in us. We are not forgiven sinners, because God's Word tells us that we are new creations in Christ, old things have passed away and all things have become new:

II Corinthians 5:17, *"Therefore if anyone is in Christ, he is a new creation: old things have passed away, behold all things have become new."*

When we accepted Jesus as our Lord and Savior and believed upon Him, we became a new creation in Christ. God's Word tells us that this new man is created in righteousness and true holiness:

Ephesians 4:24, *"And that you put on the new man, which was created according to God, in righteousness and true holiness."*
We aren't just born again, but we have also become sons (and daughters) of God:

John 1:12-13, *"But as many as received Him, to them gave the right to become the children of God, to those that believe in his name: who were born, not of blood, nor of the will of the flesh nor of the will of man, but of God."*

So what happened to the old-you? The old you was crucified with Christ. God didn't repair the old-you, He created a new-you in Christ, which is what the Bible refers to when talking about being born again:

John 3:5-7, *"**Jesus answered, Most assuredly, I say to you, unless** one is born of water and the Spirit, he cannot enter into the kingdom of God. That which is born of the flesh is flesh; and that which is born of the Spirit is spirit. Do not marvel that I said to you, you must be born again."*

Galatians 2:20, *"I have been crucified with Christ; it is no longer I who live, but Christ lives in me; and the life which I now live in the flesh I live by faith in the Son of God, who loved me and gave Himself for me."*

You are seated with Christ-a position of authority

Many people do not realize what this means. To be seated refers to a place of authority. Jesus is seated at the right hand of God, and God's Word tells us that we are seated with Christ:

Ephesians 2.6, *"And raised us up together, and made us sit together in heavenly places in Christ Jesus."*

Because of our position in Christ, we are seated in a place of authority over all sickness, diseases and demons. Jesus said that signs and wonders would follow them who believe, including casting out demons (which requires authority - see Luke 10:17-20). Look at this passage:

Mark 16:15-18, *"And he said to them, Go into all the world, and preach the gospel to every creature. He that believes and is baptized will be saved; but he who does not believe will be condemned.. And these signs will follow those that believe; In my name they will cast out demons they will speak with new tongues; They will take up serpents; and if they drink anything deadly, it will by no means hurt them; they will lay hands on the sick, and they will recover."*

Who shall these signs follow? Them that BELIEVE. That includes all true followers of Christ that are alive on the earth right now. Take a look at this passage in Revelations: Revelations 5:9-10, "And they sang a new song, saying, *You are worthy to take the scroll, and to open its seals: for You were slain, and have redeemed us to God by Your blood; out of every tribe, and tongue, and people, and nation; And have made kings and priests to our God; and we shall reign on the earth.*

The truth is, we do not need to ask God to heal somebody…we can speak with authority over that sickness and command it to flee in Jesus' name…we can command those broken bones to grow…we can command because we have authority. This was the standard practice in the early church when the followers of Christ were going out and healing the sick! The same is true when it comes to demons. We do not need to ask God to heal the sick or remove the demons, but rather we take up the authority that Christ has given us, and exercise it through faith using Jesus' name.

Did you know that the only reference to prayer for healing in the New Testament is found in James 5:15? The rest of the New Testament tells us how Jesus, His disciples and the early church would exercise their faith when they went forth to heal the sick and cast out demons.

They were not asking the Father to do it, they were saying things like, "Be healed in Jesus name" or "Rise up and walk!"

Jesus made it clear that we have authority here on earth, which is naturally ours through our position in being seated with Christ. Jesus demonstrated this when He cursed the fig tree.

Matthew 21:18-22, "Now in the morning as He returned into the city, He was hungry. And seeing a fig tree by the road, He came to it, and found nothing on it but leaves, and He said to it, Let no fruit grow on you ever again. And immediately the fig tree withered away. Now when the disciples saw it, they marveled, saying, How did the fig tree wither away so soon?

*Jesus answered and said unto them, assuredly, I say to you, If you have faith, and do not doubt, you will not only do what was done to the fig tree, but also if you say to this mountain, Be removed and cast into the sea; it will be done. And **all things**, whatever you ask in prayer, believing, you will receive."*

When we fail to realize who we are in Christ, our faith will be crippled. If you do not feel worthy to exercise your authority in Christ, then you won't be doing it in the fullness of faith and will lack assurance. Satan works diligently to program people's minds to feel unworthy and unable to walk in the power of God here on earth. This is one of the most popular strongholds in existence today in the Body of Christ! The truth is that we, by our own power and effort, are unworthy, but it is the Blood of Christ that makes us worthy. If we say we are unworthy when the blood says we are, then we are denying the work that Christ did for us on the cross!

Some of topics we will discuss later on are:

1. Our Authority in Jesus' Name
A complete discussion of our authority as a believer will be presented later. Suffice for now is to say that the very first words God spoke to man included giving man dominion over all things on the earth and in the sea, as well as, Satan and his demons. This theme also continues throughout the New Testament.

2. Generational Curses
Generational curses is a significant area of study and is not only an open door for demonic spirits, but also provides legal rights for Satan to pass down sicknesses, addictions, immorality, and much more from generation to generation. Therefore, these must be broken and the legal right removed prior to casting out the specific demon caused by a generational curse.

3. Spiritual Warfare
We will also discuss at length the need for spiritual warfare and specifically what is meant by that term. It is as much a preventative tool as it is a weapon.

Chapter Three

THE ORIGIN OF SATAN AND DEMONS

Satan:
Satan was created perfect; was full of wisdom and beauty; was an angel of protection and anointed. (Ezekiel 28:12; Isaiah 14:12-17).

Satan rebelled against God; exalted himself because of his beauty; filled himself with iniquity; and defiled the sanctuary and deceived one-third of the angels. As a consequence of his sin, he was thrown out of heaven and his final destiny is the lake of fire (II Kings 1:10-12; Ezekiel 3 8:2, 22; Rev. 20:740).

Demons
There are two generally accepted theories:
1. Demons are fallen angels: In comparing Matt. 12:24 and Matt. 25:4 1 you can only conclude that the prince of demons is the devil, and his angels are demons.

2. Demons are spirits of a race that existed before the creation of Adam. The scripture used for this theory is 2 Peter 2:4. Personally, I am convinced they are fallen angels.

What Are Demons?

They are evil spirits that are part of a highly organized Satanic kingdom on earth and in the heavenlies. The kingdom is ruled by Satan and has a specific hierarchy of power.

Demons are evil personalities and enemies of God and man. Their objectives in humans are to tempt, deceive, accuse, condemn, pressure, defile, resist, oppose, control, steal, afflict, kill and destroy. Read Ephesians 6:12 and Matthew 12:24-27 which shows the organization of Satan's kingdom. This satanic hierarchy is discussed in detail in Chapter Sixteen.

The work and activity of demonic spirits fall into three categories:

1. Those that affect the physical body
2. Those the affect our mind and emotions
3. Those that affect us spiritually

Descriptions Of Demons

A. <u>They have personalities</u>: They have names, emotions, a will and they can speak.
"Now in the synagogue there was a man who was possessed by an unclean demon and he cried out with a loud (deep, terrible) voice. Saying, let us alone! What have we to do with You (what do we have in common), Jesus of Nazareth? Did You come to destroy us? I know who You are—the Holy One of God!" (Luke 4:33-34).

B. <u>They are spirits</u>: They are evil, unclean spirits usually named according to their functions or manifestations, such as a deaf and dumb spirit (Mark 9:17-25).

Characteristics of Demons

1. Earthly demons prefer to inhabit bodies (Rev. 18:2; Matt. 12:43-44; Mark 5:12)
2. Demons live and work together---observation
3. Demons have intellect and will (Matt. 12:43-45; Mark 5:6-12)
4. Demons vary in levels of wickedness (Mail, 12:43-45; Mark 5:6-12).
5. Demons vary in power and endurance (Matt. 12:43-45; Mark5:6-12)
6. Demons require rest (Matt. 12:43-45; Mark 5:6-12)
7. Some demons only come out through prayer and fasting (Matt. 17:21; Mark 9:29)
8. Demons recognize that Jesus is the Son of God and they can also discern if people are legitimately using the authority of Jesus Christ.

Capabilities of Demons

1. They can travel (Matt. 12:43-45)
2. They cause sickness, disease, fever, physical abnormalities, mental torment, and alterations of voice
3. They can fight with God's angels (Dan. 10:13,20; Rev. 12:7)
4. They can influence human events (Rev 16:13-14)
5. They can speak through a person's voice and see through their eyes (Acts 19:15)
6. They are able to influence emotions, thoughts and actions of their host towards destruction. Examples would be the Gerasene demonic cutting himself in Mark 5:5 and the boy who was being thrown into the fire in Mark 9:22.
7. They can invigorate people with extraordinary strength (Acts 19:16) Although rare in deliverance we have experienced the unbelievable strength of a demon possessed person on two separate occasions.
8. They can deceive people and draw them away from the truth (2 Chronicles 18:20-22; Luke 4:1-13; James 1:14 inferred; and Acts 5:3).

How Jesus Dealt With Demons?

There are five important points in Mark 1:23-39 that illustrate how Jesus dealt with demons:

1. Jesus dealt with the demon and not with the man.
2. Jesus expelled the demon from the man and not the man from the synagogue.
3. Jesus was not ashamed of interruptions because this was His ministry.
4. It is reasonable to assume that the man was a member of the synagogue, but no one knew he needed deliverance; or they did but no one knew what to do.
5. It was such a dramatic confrontation that Jesus' fame and reputation spread throughout the region.

Chapter Four

CAN A CHRISTIAN HAVE A DEMON

Although it is used in scripture frequently, I purposely did not use the term possessed because most people believe it refers to someone under the total control of demonic spirits. But, the literal meaning of the word possessed simply means that an individual's personality and actions are influenced by an evil demonic spirit. (Reference: Holman Bible Dictionary). But because the term possession implies complete control to some, I use the term "have a demon" or have an "indwelling evil spirit".

Can a Christian have a demon? The simple answer is yes, believer's can be oppressed, depressed, hindered, influenced and suffer the infestation by demonic spirits. Yes a Christian can have a demon; and there are numerous instances in scripture to support this statement. For example:

1. The oppressing misfortunes and physical afflictions of Job are said to be the work of Satan (Job chapters 1&2).

2. Even in the house of God there can be those possessed by unclean spirits as Mark 1:23 clearly teaches. It says; *"Now there was a man in their synagogue with an unclean Spirit"* whom Jesus set free. There is no reason to doubt that this man was a believer who had gone there to worship.

3. In Luke 13:11-16 we read where Jesus delivered a woman from a "spirit of infirmity.' This was also in the synagogue and we know she was a believer because scripture tells us she was "a daughter of Abraham."

4. Mark 1:38-39 states that Jesus went throughout Galilee casting out demons in the synagogue (where believers worshiped).

5. Jesus rebuked the fever in Peter's mother-in-law and she was healed (Luke 4:38-39). Obviously, one does not rebuke a mere rise in temperature, but He addressed Himself to a personality, a spirit causing

the fever. To support this further, Jesus uses the same term to rebuke Satan in Mark 8:33 when He spoke to Peter and said "get behind Me Satan." Jesus was speaking to the demon who was speaking through Peter. Jesus also used this same term when He addressed the demons in the paralytic man lying on a bed in Matt. 9:2; and when He delivered the demon possessed boy of a deaf and dumb spirit in Mark 9:25-27.

6. Even what we refer to as the Lord's Prayer mentions deliverance. Matthew 6:13 says; *"And do not lead us into temptation, but deliver us from the evil one.* "Jesus didn't say keep us from the evil one but deliver us from him (the evil one).

7. Probably the best scriptural example is found in Matt. 15:21-28. Jesus clearly states deliverance (the casting out of demons) is for believers when He called it "the children's bread" and initially refused deliverance to the daughter of a non-believer. This will be discussed in greater detail later in this book.

8. Matthew 7:6 says; *"Do not give what is holy to the dogs (unbelievers)."* Whatever Jesus did (heal, cast out demons, etc.) is holy.

9. Was not Judas Iscariot a believer filled with the Holy Spirit? Jesus anointed Judas just as He did the other disciples and gave them all power to heal the sick, raise the dead, cleanse the lepers and cast out demons. Jesus even calls Judas brother in Matt. 12 48.

    It was only during the last supper that the devil entered Judas who was obviously a believer. (See Matthew 10:1-8; 18-20; 40-42; Matthew12:48-50; John 13:2, 26-27; Matthew2 7:3-4)

Note: Mark 5:1-6 is an account of demon possessed man in the country of Gadarenes living in the tombs. Was he a non-believer? Possibly, but he desired to follow Jesus immediately after his deliverance; plus verse 6 says; "He saw Jesus from afar and he ran and worshiped Him." This was before he was delivered.

A Final Word About Christians and Demons

The New Testament does not make a distinction between Christians and non-Christians having demons. Thereby implying both Christians and non-Christians can have indwelling spirits. It is also true that there is no scripture that states a Christian cannot have an indwelling demon or unclean spirit.

I am often asked, "How can a demon live where the Holy Spirit lives?" The standard answer is that they cannot coexist. The Holy Spirit lives in your spirit and a demon lives in your mind, emotions and physical body.

While that statement is true it stands alone as a very weak argument. Therefore, let's see how scripture explains it.

Many believers site I Corinthians 6:19 which says; *"...do you not know that your body is the temple of the Holy Spirit..."* Yes we are the temple of the Holy Spirit, but you must remember that the temple in Jerusalem had three parts: Outer Court, Holy Place and the Holy of Holies. The presence of God dwelt in the Holy of Holies.

The three compartments of the Temple correspond to man's three-part being: body, soul and spirit. For the Christians, the human spirit corresponds to the Holy of Holies, which is the dwelling place of the Holy Spirit. The remaining part of our temple includes our soul (mind and emotions) and our physical bodies. These are where demons reside.

Jesus found defilement in the Jerusalem temple; however, the money changers and merchants with doves and cattle were not in the Holy of Holies, but in the outer courts of the temple. Jesus proceeded to "cast out" all who defiled the temple. This is a perfect analogy to deliverance.

Chapter Five

SHOULD A NON-CHRISTIAN RECEIVE DELIVERANCE?

There are two excellent reasons not to take a non-Christian through deliverance:

First, what hope would they have of keeping the demons out after deliverance? One must personally resist the devil and a non-Christian has no grounds for doing this because he isn't submitted to the Lordship of Jesus Christ. Sin is one of the open doors for demonic entrance, and someone who has not repented of his sin cannot expect to keep demons out.

Second, in Matthew 12:43-45 Jesus makes it real clear that a non-believer will most likely end-up in a worse state than he was prior to deliverance. Jesus says; *"When an unclean spirit goes out of a man, he goes through dry places, seeking rest, and finds none. Then he says, 'I will return from the house from which I came. And when he comes, he finds it empty (not filled with the things of God), swept, and put in order. Then he goes and takes with him seven other spirits more wicked then himself and they enter and dwell there; and the last state of that man is worse than the first."*

Furthermore, a person who has not accepted Jesus as his/her Lord and Savior, rarely seeks out or submits to deliverance. They have no interest in the provisions of the cross. Plus, no one in the deliverance ministry should engage in deliverance with anyone who does not realize their need and is truly seeking help.

Unless you are sure the person has a repentant heart and will follow Jesus, it is wisdom to refuse someone deliverance.

Chapter Six

HOW CAN DEMONS GAIN ACCESS?

Approximately one-thirds of Jesus' ministry was spent casting out demons; often times it was (and is today) needed for healing.

There are spiritual laws just like there are natural laws. The law of gravity, for example, both in theory and in practice says that if something falls it will continue downward until it lands on something capable of holding it. There are also spiritual laws, known as legal rights, in the spiritual realm which states that demons cannot enter without a legal right; but they also do not have to leave until that legal right is removed.

How legal rights are removed depends upon how they entered. If a demon entered through a generational curse then that curse must be broken, if they entered through sin, there must be repentance. Once the legal right is removed the demon cannot stay unless the infested person wants it to remain. More on this later.

Specific Elements That Allow Demons To Enter

A. Sin

These can be sins of omission or commission. Sin by omission is when you do not realize that what you are doing is a sin. To sin by commission is when we willfully sin, knowing it offends God.

Sins of Commission

"Do you not know that to whom you present yourselves slaves to obey, you are that one's slave whom you obey..." (Romans 6:16).

Jesus answered them, *"Most assuredly, I say to you, whoever commits sin is a slave to sin."* (John 8:34)

When people yield to particular sins often enough, even at the level of mental acceptance, demons can enter them. Actually, even one deliberate sin can open the door for a demon to enter. It does not always happen but it can, especially when repentance doesn't happen quickly.

When a person is committing a sin they hate or resent, it is no longer freedom - it is slavery. Yielding to sin always cost you more than it gives. There is a law of sowing and reaping, which states, *"whatever a man sows, this he will also reap."* Demons are assigned to make sure people reap the negative things they have sown.

Sins of Omission

God said to Cain, *"If you do well, will you not be accepted? And if you do not do well, sin lies at the door. And its desire is for you, but you should rule over it."* (Genesis 4:7)

In this passage sin is portrayed as a personality with the desire to rule over us. This is speaking of demonic powers.

Sins of omission are the main reason that demons gain access into, or back into, a Christian. We are supposed to be filled with the Holy Spirit and seeking the face of God. We are supposed to be devoted to prayer and keeping our mind on the things from above. But when we live a life contrary to the will of God, Satan knows it. This is when a demon returns to an empty vessel and says; *"I will return to the house from which I came. And when he comes finds it empty, swept, and put in order. Then he goes and takes with him seven other spirits more wicked then himself, and they enter and dwell there....."* (Matt 12: 44-45).

Demons can only re-enter when we do what we are not supposed to do. Paul said, *"Give no place to the devil."* (Ephesians 4:27). We give place to the devil when we fail to give God what truly belongs to him, in terms of our praise, our love and our adoration.

Regularly committing any sin, either by omission or commission, is an open door to unclean spirits by giving them a legal right to enter.

Such sins as lust, addictions (alcohol, drugs, tobacco, etc.), sexual immorality, theft, and other sinful habits of intemperance and immorality are frequently the cause of unclean spirits.

Also spiritual transgressions such as *prolonged* attitudes of hate, resentment, envy, jealously, pride, uncontrolled anger, unforgiveness, intolerance, lying, desire for revenge, disunity in the church, and so on are also open doors to the invasion of unclean spirits.

All sin (word, thought and deed) can become an open door. Sin is like the electric door mat at the grocery store---the pad represents sin and it opens the door for the entrance of demonic infestation.

B. <u>Doubt, Skepticism & Ridicule of Divine Things</u>
(Speaking against God or the things of God is an invitation to the devil Therefore, your thoughts can be an open door).

The possibility of becoming bound by spirits of doubt, deception and unbelief is quite probable in those individuals who persist in negative and skeptical attitudes concerning divine truth. This is not only true for those rejecting God, but those who reject any of the truth's in God's Word (healing, deliverance, baptism in the Holy Spirit, etc.).

This is also true of those who resist the ministry of, and the supernatural manifestation of, the Holy Spirit, either through anointed ministers or spirit-filled believers.

For example, King Saul became possessed by an evil spirit as a result of his persistent resistance to God's revealed will, and to David---God's anointed servant.

The apostle Paul states plainly in II Corinthians 4:4 that Satan, the god of this world, has blinded the minds of those who do not believe; those who do not receive or are skeptical of divine truths.

Scripture also says that in the last days those who do not receive truth, *"God shall send them strong delusion, that they should believe a lie; that they might be condemned who did not believe the truth but had pleasure in unrighteousness"* (2 Thess. 2:11-12; Matt. 13:10-15; I Tim. 4:1-3).

There are many adverse affects of demonic influence and invasion which result from skepticism and/or ridicule of God's Word or any of His truths. The two most common, however, seem to be the inability to concentrate on the Bible and an inability to concentrate on prayer.

C. Occult Involvement/Witchcraft/False Religions
This is a major avenue through which the powers of darkness gain access. Many individuals who receive deliverance have either been involved in some form of occult activity and witchcraft or know of its presence in their family history.

It can be as major as being a witch or warlock, being a Free Mason or as minor as unknowingly playing with an Ouija board, reading your horoscope, practicing yoga or the martial arts, reading books written by people like Edgar Casey, attending a séance, using tarot cards, or even pretending to be a fortune teller at a children's school carnival. The latter being something my wife unknowingly did when our children were little and from which she later needed deliverance

All forms of worship of other gods places you in a position of yielding yourself to demons. If you visit a witch, worship a false god, or participate in any form of occult activity you are, either directly or indirectly, making a pack with the devil. This is something that must be renounced and the demons evicted.

For a list of various types of occultism see Appendix One

D. Emotional Crisis
(Children are especially vulnerable, but this applies to adults also)

An unusually emotional experience such as a fright, prolonged and abnormal grief, unforgiveness, or a shocking traumatic experience like a child witnessing the death of a parent could allow such an invasion of spirits.

Fear, anxiety, doubt, excessive grief, and trauma can be a cause. But, most importantly, one's attitudes and thoughts are of extreme importance during a time of crisis. Anyone who is not well versed in scripture (or in the case of a child) it would be nearly impossible for them to maintain the proper attitude in a crisis or after an extremely hurtful offense.

There are documented cases of individuals who have prolonged negative attitudes harboring guilt, and holding resentment and bitterness during difficult or traumatic experiences who were invaded by demonic spirits.

E. Hurts and Wounds From Others
Whenever someone fails to deal properly with the offenses, by forgiving them completely, they open the door to demons. Spirits of resentment, rejection, anger, hatred and bitterness are common among those who have received hurtful blows but have not forgiven those that offended them.

The key is to forgive them and avoid speaking evil of them.

F. Generational Curses
These are sometimes referred to as familiar spirits. I have written an entire chapter about generational curses. It is a very interesting topic and plays a major role in the deliverance process; plus it helps in identifying specific demons that need to be removed, and possible areas that need prayer for physical healing.

The first scripture most people use to argue against generational curses is Galatians 3:10 which says; "Christ has redeemed us from the curse of the law..." indeed He has and we are no longer under the curse of the law. However, we are still under the affects of generational curses. If we were not, people would not suffer as they do from torment, sickness and disease, depression, addictions, and the list is almost endless.

In the Old Testament curses would go on indefinitely because there was nothing one could do about it. Today we can break the curse(s) and when necessary remove any unclean spirits associated with the curse.

The other way of understanding Galatians 3:13 is to realize that this verse actually does not apply to Generational Curses. This is because the curse of the law spoken of here is sin and death and not curses.

G. Transfer Spirits

Demonic spirits can be transferred from one person to another by the laying on of hands. I Timothy 5:22 says; *"Do not lay hands on anyone hastily..."* When a person lays hands on another, the law of contact and transmission comes into operation. Through this law, the power of God or the power of the enemy can be transferred. Remember, Moses and Elijah transferred anointing and wisdom to Joshua and Elisha respectively, through the laying on of hands.

We have not only seen this but I was a recipient of a demonic spirit transferred from a woman I was praying for. Therefore, before you lay hands on anyone, or allow them to lay hands on you, protect yourself with the blood of Jesus and forbid any transference of evil spirits.

Also, make sure that anyone who lays hands on you is walking in integrity and holiness, regardless of who they are.

H. Self-Imposed Curses

Idle words are dangerous. The Word of God teaches that the power of life and death are in the tongue. Sometimes we curse ourselves with our own mouth, giving place to unclean spirits.

We may have said things like, "I am always sick" or "my kids sure are stupid" or "Jimmy sure is a poor reader." These spoken words impose curses and are open doors to the enemy.

There was a woman who worked for us who one day came in and said, "This is a bad year for the flu, and I know I am going to get it." She stated that for three days in a row and on the fourth day she called in sick. Well, she asked for it and the devil was more than happy to oblige.

Through prayer and repentance we need to close those open doors and cancel the legal rights the enemy has in the life of that person or ourselves.

> *"But I say to you that for every idle word that men speak, they will give account of it in the Day of Judgment. For by your words you will be justified and by your words you will be condemned."* Matt. 12:36-37

Self-imposed curses are an open door to spirits of fear, anxiety and stress.

I. <u>Soul Ties</u> (Usually either sexual or emotional)
Wrong relationships with unbelievers, fraudulent business practices, and adulterous relationships, committing sins of temperance or immorality are open doors to the enemy. Manipulation and control also fit into this category.

*For a complete discussion on soul ties see Chapter 19.

J. <u>Books, Videos and Music</u>
Many books, movies and music are consecrated to the devil before being distributed. As a result, anyone who listens to that type of music or watches those movies or has read those books, opens doors to demons. This is closely related to the category on occult activity and witchcraft.

K. <u>Mental Control</u>
Some individuals allow others to hypnotize them, thereby controlling their mind. Others practice telepathy to try and gain psychic powers. Because this allows the mind to become passive, these activities offer a wide open door to unclean spirits.

L. <u>Idols and Cursed Objects</u>
Any object associated with idolatry can bring demons into a person's life. One needs o be careful about bringing back, or accepting as gifts, trinkets from third world countries that may be associated with other gods, fetishes or magic in any way. Any object with supposed occultic power brings demons into the home and lives of the owner. Things as simple as symbols like the Ying and Yang, the upside-down broken cross used in witchcraft and the "Peace" movement all have demonic connotations and can bring demonic influences into your life.

M. Passivity

After nearly twenty-seven years of intense involvement in the deliverance ministry, I believe one of the most common "gates" through which demons gain access is "passivity". This gate is opened when one is not active in his Christian faith and is complacent, indifferent and lazy; when one's will is neither activated to follow Christ, to crucify the flesh or to resist the devil.

We are expected to actively love, worship and serve God. *"You shall love the Lord your God with all your heart, with all your soul and all your might."* (Deut. 6:5)

This is a major challenge for the deliverance ministry. If they remain passive and they choose not to become aggressive in their walk with Christ, deliverance would be useless, if not damaging.

Chapter Seven

SATAN'S ATTACKS BY INTRUSION

In addition to the previously discussed methods (legal rights) Satan uses to gain entrance, he also attacks by intrusion from the outside; which can also lead to demonic strongholds.

We previous discussed how demons enter through legal rights, but during our past 27 years of experience in the deliverance ministry we have discovered five primary ways that Satan also attacks by intrusion to defeat the Christian. The difference between intrusion and legal rights is that intrusion comes from the outside rather than the inside.

Demonic attacks from the outside attempt to distract us, turn our thoughts in a different direction, entice us to accept another philosophy, convince us to believe a lie, or even to look at something from a perspective other than God's.

Did you realize that a lion will never attack an animal that remains within the heard? The lion just follows the heard and waits for one of the animals to become separated.

Satan's attacks by intrusion can occur at anytime in a Christian's life. However, most frequently it will occur when you allow yourself to become separated from fellow believer's for whatever reason. And if his intrusion into your life is allowed (if it is not met with spiritual warfare) it will cause you to miss much of what God intends for your life.

What specifically does it mean when Satan intrudes into your life? Intrusion is any occasion in which Satan shoots his fiery darts or hits with a "low blow" in any of life's circumstances and then runs away. It is when you have not given him a just cause, a legal right, to have access into your life. He just intrudes and he has no right to be there.

Satan may bring you a negative or tempting thought, symptoms of an illness, or any number of things. He hates when you worship God so he will often try and intrude on your prayer time. His purpose is always to interrupt your fellowship with God or disrupt your focus on God with the intent of causing you to focus on your difficult or distressing circumstances.

Satan's goal is to destroy you, to bring you down, to keep you in the dark, and to make you ineffective. His attacks are designed to keep you from being all that God created you to be. He wants you uninformed or misinformed about the kingdom of darkness unaware of his intrusions into your life; unaware that you are even engaged in a fight; and unaware or misinformed about indwelling demonic spirits, legal rights, and the ministry of deliverance.

Strategy 1: Lies and Deception.
One of the biggest lies Satan uses to deceive us and keep us in bondage is to convince you that a Christian cannot have a demon. If Satan can use this lie to deceive you then he can keep you in bondage to whatever it is he is using to torment you: sickness & disease, emotional hurts, unforgiveness, doubt and unbelief, addictions, and the list is endless.

Another major deception is to place the blame on God for the consequences of ancestral sins. Frequently we have encountered men and women who have been sexually abused. Often they will inform us that someone in the family knew about it but did nothing. They became angry with God for not protecting them; for not keeping them out of harm's way.

They are simply unaware of generational curses. Once they are reminded that God cannot lie; and that He said He would visit the sins of those that hate Him in future generations (those ancestor's who did not love, worship or serve God) then they understand why God could not protect them. But these curses can be broken and the individual set free through deliverance.

Satan never just walks into your life and announces that He is going to set up a stronghold. He begins to gradually feed lies into your mind which will eventually destroy you. He knows that if we believe his lies then he has power over us.

You may know the truth in your mind but still live out a lie in your daily experience, because knowing something in your mind doesn't necessarily enable you to live it. "Knowing the truth" is not knowing theological doctrine but rather intimacy with the Truth...who is Jesus Christ!

<u>Following are some common lies, many of which we were trained up in from a child:</u>
1. We get rich by getting all that we can, keeping every bit of it, and not letting anyone else have any of it. We learn that the world's way to riches is greed and selfishness. Contrary to this lie, Jesus said that in order to be rich, you must give it away. Jesus told the rich young ruler: *"If you want to be perfect, go, sell all you have and give it to the poor, and you will have treasure in heaven; and come, follow Me."* Matthew 19:21.
2. To be first you must get ahead of everyone else. You must get there before they get there, and maintain your position by whatever means is necessary. Yet Jesus said if you want to be first, then choose to be last. Our attitudes and our actions reveal who we really are and what we really believe. "We practice daily all that we believe and all else is religious talk!!"
3. You must find yourself by looking deep inside until you discover the true you. But the truth says that if you want to find yourself you must give your life away to others.
4. You are to seek self-fulfillment and your own happiness at all cost, ignoring the needs of others. But Truth says that to really live, you must first die to yourself.

These are some of the lies and thought patterns Satan uses to set up what can become demonic strongholds.

Strategy 2: <u>Accusations and Condemnation.</u>
Has the devil ever whispered in your ear: "You'll never amount to anything." "You're worthless." "You're useless." "You're no good." "You're dumb." "Nobody likes you." "Nobody wants to be your friend." "You'll never get married." "Your spouse doesn't love you." We could all add to this list.

If you begin to entertain those thoughts you give the devil a foothold into your life. Therefore, do not listen to the devil's lies and accusations against you. When Satan begins to whisper such lies tell him that isn't who God says I am. Then begin to tell Satan who you are in Christ.

If you sin, and are receiving conviction from the Lord, then you need to repent before God.

There is a difference between Satan's condemnation and your sin. If you sin, you must repent and turn from that sin to God; thanking Him that Jesus has already forgiven and cleansed you.

But never see yourself as sinful and condemned, or you will "live it out" and continue to walk in sin. This is what Satan wants you to do. You need to see yourself as God sees you. If you are unaware of who you are in Christ, start a systemic study of scripture and discover just how awesome God thinks you are.

Strategy 3: Doubt, Unbelief and Fear
Have you even been shot down by Satan by him telling you that you don't have enough faith to believe that God loves you enough to do something good for you? God heals everyone else, but not me. He supplies money for everyone else, but not me. God help's others with their marriage, but He hasn't taken care of mine.

Do you fail to pick up the shield of faith because you don't believe God loves you enough to provide for your needs? Do you fail to trust Him?

These thoughts are not your own, they are an intrusion of the enemy into your thought process. Don't let the enemy defeat you with doubt, unbelief and fear.

The process is simple: (I) Read and belief God's Word, and (2) Evaluate your every thought and if it doesn't line up with God's Word, reject it.

Strategy 4: The Battle of the Mind
There is a constant battle in your mind between the Holy Spirit and Satan. Satan wants to control your mind. You can stop him from doing so by not

letting your mind run wild when Satan attacks you.

We are to bring every thought into obedience, captive to Jesus Christ. Scripture says to take every thought captive and to pull down every high thing that exalts itself against the knowledge of God.

"For though we walk in the flesh, we do not war after the flesh; For the weapons of our warfare are not carnal, but mighty through God to pulling down strongholds; Casting down imaginations and every high thing that exalts itself against the knowledge of God, and bringing every thought into captivity to the obedience of Christ." 2 Corinthians 10:3-4

Don't ever worry about inappropriate or evil thoughts passing through your mind. You have not sinned. Just bring those thoughts into captivity. It is only when you "hang on" to those inappropriate or evil thoughts, and entertain them, pamper them, and encourage them have you sinned in your mind.

When Satan throws his wicked thoughts your way, whether they are thoughts of adultery, lust, self-pity, judgment, jealously, or whatever, pull those thoughts down and bring them into captivity.....give them to Jesus. If you fail to do that, those thoughts will take root in you, and soon you will find yourself in bondage to sin.

Strategy 5: Attacking the Word of God
After Jesus was baptized He was led into the wilderness, by the Holy Spirit, where Satan tempted Him using God's Word in an attempt to ensnare Him. Each time Jesus countered with a rebuttal; "It is written."Satan was trying to use the Word against Jesus by taking it out of context (see Luke 4:9-11). But Jesus refused to have a dialog with Satan and said, *"Thou shall not tempt the Lord your God"* (Luke 4:12)

If you know God's Word then the devil cannot attack you with it by taking it out of context, which is one of his tactics.

Chapter Eight

TIHE WORK AND ACTIVITY OF DEMONIC SPIRITS

Demonic spirits fall into three categories: Those which affect our physical body, those that affect our mind and emotions, and those that effect us spiritually.

Physical Infirmities

Infirm Spirits: This category includes an infinite variety of spirits ranging from those that act upon the spinal cord, muscles, or brain causing deformity, lameness, etc.; to spirits causing asthma, cancer, tumors, paralysis, migraine headaches, insomnia, tuberculosis, epilepsy, and so on.

Sometimes these are organic afflictions and sometimes they are caused by a specific demon. In either cast they are demonic since we know that all sickness is the "oppression" (or work) of Satan (Acts 10:38).

Dumb Spirits: This spirit paralyzes the speech facilities and causes one to become mute (without speech). In Matthew 9:32-33, we are told that the dumb man possessed a demon and that when the demon was cast out by Jesus the man began to speak.

Deaf Spirits: This spirit binds, or afflicts the auditory nerves, resulting in deafness. When both speech and hearing are affected, the individual is termed deaf-mute. Jesus treated such a condition as being caused by an unclean or evil spirit which He cast out. (Mark 9:25).

Blind Spirit: Blind spirits paralyze the optic nerve, in which case it wouldn't even respond to surgery. In Matthew 12:22 Jesus cured a blind and mute man who was demon possessed.

NOTE: Satan will at times afflict individuals with diseases of the ears and eyes that do not result in blindness or deafness.

Mental Oppression:
These spirits have as their primary function the assault on one's mind with evil or unclean thoughts, feelings of depression, apathy, fear and anxiety, or with temptations ranging from pride to failure.

This category includes specific spirits of insanity and suicide spirits that attempt to drive the oppressed individual to self-destruction or self-injury (Mark 9:17-22), while others cause some individuals to perform acts of shameful or anti-social behavior.

Other spirits that affect the mind cause fear, anxiety, panic, hysteria, rage, rebellion, resentment, psychological disorders, etc.

Spiritual Oppression or Delusion
Spirits that affect the mind and body seem to get the most attention, probably because they are the most noticeable. However, the most aggressive, the most intelligent, the most cunning and deceptive, and the strongest spirits are those that attack us spiritually.

Satan's basic strategy is to gain control of the lives of men and women in order to fulfill his evil purpose through them in his warfare against the kingdom of God. Therefore, the major purpose of Satan is to destroy the church and to affect and control our education, culture, social activities, and world affairs.

These spirits possess humans and control them directly or through spirit guides, mediums, fortunetellers, clairvoyants, false teachers, false prophets, and diluted religious teachers and leaders (those who teach delusion and deception).

These are often religious spirits clocked with respectability and appear as "an angel of light", or as "ministers of righteousness" (2 Cor. 11:14-15) in churches, seminaries, and their religious organizations and institutions.

MOST COMMON SYMPTOMS OF INDWELLING SPIRTS

1. Emotional Problems
   Things like resentment, hatred, fear, rejection (feeling unloved or unwanted); self-pity, jealously, worry, insecurity.

2. Mental Problems
   Disturbances in your mind or thought life such as: mental torment, procrastination, indecision, compromise, confusion, doubt, rationalization, loss of memory.

3. Speech Problems
   Outbursts or uncontrolled use of the tongue. This includes lying, cursing, blasphemy, criticism, mockery, and gossip.

4. Sexual Problems
   Recurring unclean thoughts and acts regarding sex. These include fantasy sex experiences, masturbation, lust, perversion, homosexuality, fornication, incest, and harlotry (prostitution).

5. Addictions
   The most common are nicotine, alcohol, drugs, medications, caffeine, and food.

6. Physical Infirmities
   Many diseases and physical afflictions are demonic spirits of infirmity (see Luke 13:11). When a demon of infirmity is cast out there is often a need to pray for healing of whatever damage has resulted. There is a very close relationship between deliverance and healing.

7. Religious Error
   Involvement TO ANY DEGREE in religious error can open the door for demons. Objects and literature from sources of religious error have been known to attract demons into houses.

8. <u>False Religions</u>:
   Eastern religion, pagan religions, philosophies, and mind sciences. Note that this includes some popular interest areas like yoga for exercise and karate which cannot be divorced from heathen worship.

9. <u>Christian Cults</u>:
   Mormonism, Jehovah's Witnesses, Christian Science, Unity and several others. These cults either deny or confuse the necessity of Christ's blood as the way to atonement for sin and salvation. Cults also include lodges, societies, and social agencies which use religion as a foundation, but omit the blood atonement of Jesus Christ.

10. <u>Occult and Spiritism</u>:
    Séance's, witchcraft, magic, Ouiji boards, levitation, and writing analysis, ESP, automatic handwriting, hypnosis, horoscopes, astrology, divination, etc. . .ANY method of supernatural knowledge, wisdom, guidance and power apart from God is forbidden.

11. <u>False Doctrine</u>:
    I Timothy 4:1 warns of the great increase of doctrinal errors promised by deceiving and seducing spirits in the last days. Such doctrines are designed to attack both the humanity and deity of Jesus Christ; to deny the inspiration of scripture, distract Christians from the move of the Holy Spirit, to cause confusion and disunity in the Body of Christ, etc

Chapter Nine

THE CHURCH UNDER ATTACK

This chapter has been added because the church to whom I first taught this course had been under attack for some time and as a body needed to recognize what had happened. The fact is, most Christian churches have been, and continue to be, under attack. Yet most are unaware of why it is happening.

Anytime a church has a desire to move forward and go deeper in the things of God, you get Satan's attention. In turn, you can expect to be attacked. This is especially true of leadership. It simply goes with the territory and you learn to do battle (engage in spiritual warfare) or you will be overcome. The congregation to whom I refer were familiar with how the enemy attacked the leadership in their church through a spirit of lust. But, there was much more happening at that church, and most other churches, that have a heart for the things of God.

Satan has a consistent strategy that he uses against the Christian community. The best way to describe it is to call it what it is: strife and discord. That is exactly what he had done at this church. Listen to what James says about this type of demonic attack: *"For where envy and strife is, there is confusion and every evil work"* (James 3:16).

It is important to understand that envy, strife and discord will always bring division. Therefore, it is of extreme importance that when "strife" shows up that it is dealt with quickly. If it is not, in a short period of time the church family will be divided and split by internal problems.

<u>A typical scenario</u> would be: The enemy will convince someone in the church that he/she has a view that must be acknowledged and implemented by the church leadership. Often it is simply a desire to promote one's own ideas at the exclusion of everyone else's ideas.

This is a divisive act, yet the person usually doesn't realize they are operating under the influence of an evil spirit. This type of individual usually is also being tormented by a spirit of insecurity and a spirit of pride.

Often the leadership will then implement that person's suggestion, either because the person is persistent and/or leadership is non-confrontational.

From this scenario comes strife and discord and soon the church becomes divided.

Another scenario is when there is an obvious sin going on within the local church and the leadership ignores it. This will also bring strife and discord, and before long division among church members as they began to pick sides.

In both these scenarios the end result is what the apostle James refers to as "confusion." The word confusion is taken from the word "akatastasia" and it was used in the New Testament times to describe "civil disobedience, disorder and anarchy in a city, state, or government."

This is what happens when strife and discord are allowed to persist in the local church. As people begin to ignore the legitimate authority that God has given the pastor and his elders, they move into the area of civil disobedience and disorder which will destroy the church. I have seen this happen in two churches, both of which have closed their doors.

It does not have to be that way. God has trained you, through adversity, and given you the weapons to defeat Satan and his evil army. You just need to recognize his attacks and be prepared to jump in the fight, recognizing our battle is in the spiritual realm and not against one another.

Common Demons that Attack the Church

Every effective local church will have specific demons assigned to destroy their ministry. And while it is true that any given church may have a different grouping of evil spirits attacking the church, it is also true that there are five very real and persistent demons that are usually assigned to cause misery and conflict among the congregations.

The church needs to identify what spirits are operating over and among them and wage a continual warfare against these evil spirits. But it must be remembered that our battle is not against flesh and blood (not against one another) but against that enemy of God and man, Satan.

This is not to say that a local church will have each of these spirits in operation, but these five spirits are the most common.

Quite frequently, these spirits manifest themselves through people within the same church, yet they usually do not realize the enemy is using them; others know but do not seek help.

The Spirit of Jezebel

First let me tell you about the man who married Jezebel.

I Kings 21:25 says, "There was no one like Ahab who sold himself to do wickedness in the sight of the Lord, because Jezebel his wife stirred him up."

Ahab was a king of Israel who disobeyed God's law by marrying Jezebel, the daughter of the king of Sidon. Jezebel used her power as Queen to promote the worship of the false god Baal. Baal was the god of the storm who required human sacrifices; which is satanic worship.

Ahab allowed his wife to dominate the people, and establish pagan worship, and the sacrifice of children. Ahab represents a man who is of weak spiritual character, both at home and in the church.

When you combine a Jezebel spirit and an Ahab spirit in the church you have a deadly combination.

Jezebel was King Ahab's controlling and manipulative wife (1 Kings 18:14-19). In today's society, the spirit of Jezebel is identified as a source of obsessive sensuality, a worshiper of the occult, witchcraft, and a seeker for equality of rights. Jezebel means without cohabitation: this spirit has no interest in others. She is not a team player and she is self-sufficient, controls situations, and tries to control the minds and actions of others.

Jezebel likes to monopolize and is arrogant. She controls her husband and others through sex and/or manipulation. She distains masculine authority, and is characterized by dominating and controlling her husband and church leadership instead of submitting to their leadership.

Those with a Jezebel spirit refuse to cohabit in a home or a church unless she can control and have domination over others (especially those in leadership). If she is unable to accomplish this, she changes her tactics and secretly instigates others to do evil, all while hiding behind them.

We also see this spirit in the wife of King Herod, who asked her daughter to dance in front of her husband in order to seduce him with sexual movements, and thereby accomplish her plan to kill John the Baptist.

The Jezebel spirit operates in three areas:

<u>The Human Being:</u> It operates in an individual; usually a woman but not always. It attacks both genders, but has a greater tendency towards females, who generally let themselves be dominated by jealously. The main objective of the Jezebel spirit is to control and manipulate.

<u>The Church</u>: This spirit infiltrates the church and tries to control God's servants or cause them to sin. It operates in the church as a spirit of seduction and fornication. It hates the prophetic and resists the fire of the Holy Spirit—those who are filled with the manifestations of His power.

<u>The Nation:</u> Jezebel operates as a principality over a nation, taking control and bringing its inhabitants into bondage. This took place in the nation of Israel when Ahab allowed Jezebel to dominate the country through satanic control and idolatry.

Today the battle has intensified as this spirit uses the media as a means to operate in nations. Things like newspapers, adult videos, advertising, magazines, and pornography are seducing souls, even church members and church leaders.

What Are The Characteristics of a Person Under The Influence of Jezebel?

- They often boast of revelations they have received, seeking to exalt their own ego.
- They seek recognition and like to be recognized by church leaders and become resentful if they are not.
- They try to get close to church leadership through flattery and compliments.
- They seek prophecies that will elevate them to a higher position in front of others.
- They rarely want to be in authority, but prefer to be the "power behind the throne."

A Pharisaic Spirit

This spirit is filled with deadly hostility. It killed Ahab, crucified Jesus, stoned Stephen, and tried to destroy Paul. This spirit hates grace and loves legalism. This spirit wars against true worship and our relationship with God.

How do you know when this spirit is in operation?

- Their love for the Lord is lost or diminished.
- They lose their hunger for the things of God.
- They become insensitive to the presence of God.
- They become insensitive to the needs of God's people.
- Their prayer life becomes routine.

Lukewarm believers are vulnerable to the enemy and can be used by him at any moment. One must repent and ask the Lord for forgiveness.

The Spirit of Witchcraft

This spirit controls through fear and men's traditions. It is closely related to the spirit of Jezebel. The goal of this spirit is to destroy teachings of the Bible and subsequently, Christian life. The spirit of witchcraft uses force and emotional power to manipulate others. Examples of this spirit working in individuals would include:

* Manipulating, controlling prayers.
* Using fear to get people to serve or not to leave the church.
* Condemning messages to cause others to feel bad.
* Sowing seeds of division among the people of God.

The Spirit of Absalom

This is a spirit of treason and often times operates in the hearts of church leaders. Absalom was a son of David who betrayed him by leading Israel into a rebellion against him in order to take over his throne and power. This spirit operates through church leaders or other members who are unhappy and offended. This person seeks others who will back their agendas, which usually are contrary to the vision of the pastor or other church leadership.

This spirit often leads it's followers to leave the church, causing division and bringing chaos.

The spirit of Absalom, like Jezebel, likes attention and is consumed with the desire to control. It is independent and likes to promote itself.

The major cause of this spirit is personal ambition. Unhappy leaders want to be first and to promote their own agenda ahead of the local churches agenda.

This spirit usually targets elders, deacons, members of church boards or those on influential committees.

Chapter Ten

SIGNS OF DEMONIC HARASSMENT AND OPPRESSION

Could be from an indwelling spirit but may be just what we call harassment or oppression.

This is not necessarily an all-inclusive list but general categorical signs that can be easily recognized. Individuals in this category may or may not need deliverance. But for sure they need to engage in spiritual warfare (a later topic of discussion).

The person feels seduced: Demons persuade people to do bad things. This is something we have all experienced. This is not to say you can get away with "the devil made me do it" because you have a free will to make the right or wrong choice. But demons will do everything they can to influence you and they can be very convincing.

When someone says; "I didn't even realize what I was doing, nor did I see the danger." This indicates that they are being seduced by an evil influence.

For example: If someone finds a purse with money inside and immediately hears a voice saying: "Take it, nobody will know, others would take it." This is one way the enemy will try and persuade a person to sin.

The person fasts and prays without results: All too often I have heard believers say, "I have prayed, fasted, rebuked, gone to counseling, seen a psychologist, and tried to bind spirits. Yet something that seems stronger than me keeps making me do whatever it is they shouldn't do.

The person feels harassed: Demons study you. They observe and learn your weaknesses. Just when you think everything is under control, in a moment of discouragement the enemy springs a trap to harass you and tries to make you fall into some sort of sin. For example: using bad language on the golf course after a bad shot.

Chapter Eleven

SIGNS OF DEMONIC INFESTATION

Individuals who experience these signs are definitely candidates for deliverance.

<u>The person feels tormented</u>: Matthew 18:34-35 says; "In anger his master turned him over to the jailers to be tortured, until he should pay back all he owed. This is how My Heavenly Father will treat each of you unless you forgive your brother from your heart."

<u>Many believers are tormented by demons for the simple reason that they have not forgiven.</u>

What does demonic torture in a person actually mean?

It can be either a physical or spiritual torment. Therefore, let us look at both.

<u>Physically</u>:
The person may suffer physical afflictions such as arthritis, ulcers, paralysis, asthma, etc. This is not to say that all these diseases are demonic, but often they are the product of demons and the result of unforgiving others.

When we were in the mission field we were asked to minister to a woman who was in so much pain from arthritis she could not wear shoes and shuffled her feet to walk across the room. It was too painful for her to get dressed so she wore P.J.'s and a robe.

We discovered she had developed all these symptoms after her husband left her for another woman. After some ministry she forgave her husband and received deliverance for a spirit of bitterness and unforgiveness and then we prayed for her healing.

Nothing seemed to change. But one week later that same woman walked up two flights of stairs in high heel shoes to attend a Bible Study in our home and during worship she was dancing in our living room...completely healed.

Tormenting spirits can be physically debilitating, but we have the authority to remove their legal right(s) and cast them out.

<u>Spiritually</u>: An example would be a person who suffers from guilt because they committed a sin, such as murder, abortion, abuse, adultery, and each of us could add to the list. A spirit of guilt can torment a person relentlessly.

<u>The person develops compulsive desires.</u> There is no word that more specifically describes demonic activity than "compulsive." Usually, behind every compulsive desire or behavior there is a demon or demonic influence.

People may say, "I have an overwhelming desire to smoke, drink alcohol, use drugs, overeat, steal, sexual addictions, etc." Often they will say, "I have tried to stop, but something is just pushing me to do it and I can't stop." This is a sign of demonic influence in that person's life.

<u>A sense of enslavement</u>: Suppose for example you committed a sexual sin and then repented with all your heart. You know God forgave you and justified you, but you still feel an intense desire to do it again. Why? Because there is a demonic influence. Demons can cause addictions of all kinds.

<u>Physical attacks</u>: Demons can cause physical symptoms, such as chronic fatigue, sleep disorders, psychological disorders, physical abnormalities, and depression, to mention just a few.

<u>Emotional and Psychological Hurts:</u> This is when a person experiences emotions of rejection, abandonment, resentment, insecurity, self-pity, guilt and so forth. These hurts and accompanying emotions rise up whenever you think about a certain past experience. When this happens you can be assured that it is demonic. We will discuss these in greater detail later on.

Mental Oppression: As we mentioned previously, this is when one's mind is assaulted with thoughts of depression, fear, anxiety, thoughts of pride or failure, unclean thoughts, etc. This category also includes suicide, insanity, and anti-social behavior.

Areas Affected By Demon Spirits

1. The Emotions: Unclean spirits can reside in the heart of a man and damage his emotions with feelings of rejection, anger, hatred, and dispute.

2. The Body: Unclean spirits inhabit certain parts of the body. For example, sexual spirits often reside in the eyes, while other spirits reside in various places throughout the physical body.

" And there was a woman there who for eighteen years had an infirmity caused by a spirit (a demon spirit of sickness) . She was bent completely forward and utterly unable to straighten herself up or to look forward. And when Jesus saw her, He called (her to Him) and said to her, Woman you are released from your infirmity! Then He laid (His) hands on her, and instantly she was made straight, and she recognized and thanked and praised Him.

3. The Tongue: Evil thoughts originate in the heart, and out of the abundance of the heart, the mouth speaks.

"Brood of vipers! How can you, being evil, speak good things? For out of the abundance of the heart the mouth speaks. A good man out of the good treasure of his heart brings forth good things, and an evil man out of the evil treasure brings forth evil things. But I say to you that for every idle word men may speak; they will give account of it on the Day of Judgment. For by your words you will be justified, and by your words you will be condemned." Matthew 12:34-37.

Some people seem to always be talking negatively; they criticize, murmur, and complain. Some people curse or gossip or use their tongue to hurt and degrade others. The point being that anytime a person speaks something other than a language of worship or blessing, it is demonically influenced.

4. Appetite: Some spirits affect the appetite, such as gluttony and anorexia.

5. Sex: Spirits of lust, adultery, homosexuality and fornication seek control over many people. These spirits do not travel alone; they work together in gangs; which is true of many demonic spirits. We will see this clearly when we discuss spirit groupings.

Chapter Twelve

GENERATIONAL CURSES
(A Look in the Mirror)

The purpose of this chapter is to help you grasp the fact that generational curses are real and they are an open door to demons.

We are going to spend a significant amount of time discussing generational curses because it is a major avenue for demons to gain access. Yet, it is a topic that is seldom taught and most believers have little or no understanding of its significance.

One of the things we tell people prior to deliverance is that the need for deliverance is not your fault. . .It is not something you did but something that was done to you.

Deliverance is one of God's gifts for defeating Satan and setting you free from these tormenting demons.

Generational curses are real, yet there are some in the church, and even those in full-time ministry, who do not believe curses exist. But Scripture tells us that God will punish those who disobey Him.

"You shall not bow down to them or serve them. For I, the Lord your God, am a jealous God visiting the iniquity of the fathers upon the children to the third and forth generations of those who hate Me." Exodus 20:5

Turn your Bibles to Deut. Chapter 28:
Have you ever looked in a mirror and thought I am starting to look like my father or my mother?

The truth is we get a lot more from our father, our father's father, our father's brother, our mother, our mother's mother, our father's, father's father and so—we get a lot more than most people can even imagine. The fact is, we have all received a trunk load of junk from your ancestors.

And many of these things have allowed Satan to enter into our lives. No one is exempt so what you read in the following pages applies directly to your life.

Exodus 20: says; *"I the Lord your God, am a jealous God, visiting the iniquity of the fathers on the children to the third and fourth generations of those who hate Me"* (those who disobey Me--those who sin).

In Deuteronomy 28: 1-14 there are 28 blessings for being obedient to God. In Deuteronomy 28: 15-68 there are 112 curses for being disobedient to God.

There are a wide variety of curses ranging from cancer and heart disease to female problems, boils, tumors, mental problems and suicide— 112 in all plus "every sickness and plague which is not written in this book of the law..." (Verse 61).

<u>Please read verses 45, 46, 58-59, and 61</u>
The principle of Generational Curses is also called spiritual determinism and is carried out by demons. They usually manifest in tendencies within families. Things like addictions to drugs, alcohol or tobacco; sickness and disease like cancer and heart disease; emotions like anger, resentment, revenge and bitterness; other things like divorce and sexual immorality; and finally things that we think are our own personality traits like timidity (shyness) or control—any extreme personality traits.

Before we really get into this topic let me clear up something that often causes confusion when discussing curses. According to Galatians 3:13, we are redeemed from the curse. Jesus became a curse on our behalf. Specifically, it says; "Christ has redeemed us from the curse of the law, having become a curse for us." Since this is true than how can a Christian still be under a curse?

First of all that verse refers to the curse of the law which is the law of sin and death and not generational curses. And even if it did apply to generational curses, we are all still under the effects of the curse. In the Old

Testament there was nothing that could be done. But today we have Jesus and these curses can be broken and lifted from us and our descendants. Unfortunately, most Christians aren't even aware that the things they struggle with are generational curses nor do they know how to deal with them.

"Redeem" means to buy back, to pay the debt in full. In order to understand redemption, we need to understand that it is legally ours because Jesus gave it to us, but that we have to appropriate this gift in order to experience it.

To really understand this we need to know the difference between what is legally ours and what is experientially ours. Just because something is legally ours does not mean we automatically obtain it or walk in the freedom of it. Plus we have an adversary, the devil, whose goal is to keep us from what is legally ours.

If the devil can keep you ignorant of what is legally yours and how to obtain it, he can still enforce a curse against you (anything from sickness and disease to addictions, foul language, and pornography— whatever you struggle with).

The promises of God are not automatic. We are (have been) healed by the stripes of Jesus but to obtain it the believer has to appropriate it (pray believing) and continue to battle and stand in the promise.

The Good News of Jesus Christ has made a provision for us to win—to appropriate the promise and gain victory over the curse and the effects of that curse.

Simply put---Curses have to be broken over the life of the believer, and they must learn how to stand in faith against those curses, keeping them from operating in their life.

<u>Generational Curses and Blessings Are Not Some New Idea...</u>
Matt. 27:25 says that Pilate washed his hands of the matter because he found no fault in Jesus. . .But the Jews cried out "let His blood be on our heads and

the heads of our children"...they knew that the fault would not stop with them---but would be passed down to their descendants. And that is exactly what has happened.

What is a Generational Curse?

The world says it like this, "Like father, like son". The medical profession calls it hereditary; and the Word of God says it this way, "The iniquity of the father passes on from generation to generation".

A curse is recompense (payment) in the life of a person and his or her descendants as a result of iniquity. Scripture says a curse causes sorrow of heart and gives demonic spirits legal entry into a family whereby they can carry out their wicked plans. (Lamentations 3:64-66).

Another way to describe your life under a curse is adversity. This includes adverse circumstances, misfortune, continual struggle, difficulty, hard life, bad times, ups and downs, bitter pill, slump, depression, need, bad luck, rotten deal; and the list goes on.

A person under a curse (you and me) is a person under siege.

Another way to describe a generational curse is to say it is a Doorway for Demons. Curses open the door for demon spirits to enter and operate. These evil spirits can operate in families from generation to generation. *One of the major keys to a successful deliverance is understanding and breaking curses.*

Most spirits will not come out of people until curses are broken because curses give them legal entry, and they use curses as a legal right to remain. There are spiritual laws in the spirit realm just like there are natural laws in our realm of existence.

God's answer to a curse is deliverance. The problem is a curse and the solution is deliverance.

Please understand I am not teaching you anything that isn't found in God's Word.

I just mentioned that a curse is recompense or payment or an adversity on a person and his descendants as a result of an iniquity. Therefore, in order to understand generational curses, you need to know the difference between sin and iniquity.

We often use these words (sin & iniquity) interchangeably but it is not sin that passes down the blood line, it is the curse (a sin was committed and a curse began). A curse is the penalty of sin, or the effect of sin. It is the pollution released into your life because of sin (yours or the sins of your ancestors).

A recompense is a reward or a payment. Just as the Lord rewards righteousness, He also rewards sin, He rewards sin in the form of a curse. We must, therefore, recognize when we have a propensity toward a certain sin or sins.

At the end of this message I will lay out a simple method of identifying and breaking generational curses; which is the whole purpose of this chapter.

Let me make this idea of iniquity real simple...iniquities are second nature sins...what does that mean?

- We are drawn to them—like a duck has a propensity for water.

- We realize that for others this "whatever" doesn't seem to be a big problem; but for us we can't walk away from it. Iniquity is not sin, it is the propensity to commit sin.

Examples would include:
1. Alcoholism
2. Gambling
3. Pornography
4. Tobacco
5. Financial problems
6. Drugs like pot, heroin, etc.
7. Depression

8. Chronic sickness or disease (i.e. chronic bronchitis)
9. Abuse of or by other people
10. Timidity (thinking it is just your personality)
11. Premature death

A generational curse is like a genetic defect carried through our DNA but it is demonic.

If you don't have a propensity (aren't drawn to) something someone else has we often say things like, "why don't they just quit (smoking, drinking, cursing, etc). Look at gambling: one person can go to a casino with a $20.00 limit, lose it and quit. Another person, with an iniquity of gambling, will set the same limit but continue to keep going back to the banker for more chips. Some may go so far as to sell their car or home and end up losing their family because of gambling.

These curses pass from generation to generation until someone figures out how to stop the curse and then sometimes it requires deliverance of that spirit to keep it from remaining in your life.

When Jesus was walking with His disciples they asked if the man was blind for something he did or for something his parents did. Jesus didn't rebuke them for asking a foolish question because they understood curses. They understood the Old Testament where it says; "The fathers have eaten sour grapes but the children are set on edge." In other words, the fathers have done something wrong but the children pay the price.

One of the greatest scriptures found in God's Word is found in Matthew chapter 16 where Jesus asks His disciples, "Who do men say that I am?" And they said, "Some say this and some say that." Then Jesus said "But who do you say I am?"

If you fully understand Peter's response you realize this is the basis for everything. Peter's response was a Jewish response, a Hebrew response. He said, "You are the Christ" which in Hebrew means "the anointed One of God who will remove the burden and break the yoke." The burden is the wages of sin---death. The yoke is the curse that passes from generation to generation because of sin. Jesus is not only the one who forgives us of our sin but He also breaks (actually lifts from us) every generational curse.

Examples in the Bible of Iniquity Passed Through the Generations:

The First Murder
- Genesis 4:8 tells the story of Cain being jealous of Abel and killing him.
- In Genesis 4:23 we read of Cain's 4th generation descendant, Lameck, who says, "I have killed a man for wounding me, even a young man for hurting me." (In fact, I think I read where the bible calls him a wild man).
- The iniquity multiplies---it gets worse each time it crops up in a descendant.

What Was King David Thinking?
- David is out for an evening stroll and heads to the rooftop
- Sees a beautiful women bathing across the way
    + Lust over takes him
    + It's all he can think about
    + He knows it's wrong
    + He summons her to his quarters
    + He was the King- he has so much
    + But lust made his desire more than he could handle
    + Why?
    + Rahab was his great, great great grandmother and she was a prostitute (harlot) before she was set free from that life and began to follow the one true God.
- Lust and sexual sin was in David's spiritual DNA
  Solomon was David's son and we read in the Scriptures that as wise as he was in many things:
    1. His lust for women is what led to his destruction.
    2. He married foreign women and allowed them to bring their idols into the kingdom.

And Then There Was The Curse of Canaan
- Genesis 6:9 tells us that Noah was a just man, perfect in the generations.
- He walked with God.
- Then along came his son Ham.
- Noah was asleep in his tent
- Ham uncovered his father's nakedness and bragged about it to his two brothers outside the tent
- Ham had homosexual tendencies.
- When Noah realized what had taken place, he was so humiliated and angry that he curses Hams son, Canaan, saying "What is in you will be full blown in him."
- When we study the Canaanites you will discover that they settle in Sodom—a town known for homosexuality.
- The curse was fulfilled in Canaan.

How About Those Ungodly Amorites?
- Genesis 15:16 says; "But in the 4th generation, your descendants will come back here, for the iniquity of the Amorites has not received its full measure."
- The Amorites were known for idol worship/child sacrifice and prostitution.

Let me share a story of a Generational Curse that was reported in the newspaper (the paper didn't give his name so we'll call him John). John had met another prisoner there that was in the cell right next to his. They had become friends and he had observed first hand---his anger and rebellion toward authority. He was a "lifer without parole" because of fatally shooting a police officer during an armed robbery.

Because of overcrowding in that particular prison—John was unexpectedly transferred to another prison. To John's amazement—there, across the aisle in another cell—was a man who was the spitting image of the prisoner he had befriended and just left at the other prison. The only difference was the age—this prisoner was much younger—but the mannerism, the rage toward the guards—it was a mirror image.

John began to talk to the young man—he couldn't have been more than 35—but the similarities were uncanny. Finally, John got up the nerve to ask his last name---it was not the same as the other prisoner he was comparing him to.

He explained to the young man that he had met someone in another prison that looked so much like him and had some of the same characteristics---but they didn't have the same name so they couldn't be related. The young man replied that isn't necessarily true. He said I never knew my real dad. The last time I saw him I was just a baby. My Mom said he was no good and my step dad adopted me. She thought that would be the best for me since my dad was such a loser and probably would end up killing someone and spending the rest of his life in prison.

"What a joke! Look how that turned out—I was in a convenience store and just needed a bottle of beer. I wasn't like robbing the place or anything, I just wanted a beer. I think the kid would have given it to me and everything would have been ok—but then in through the front door comes John Law and the kid at the counter gave him some sort of sign. The cop drew his gun and told me to put my hands up—Me? Put my hands up for a cop? He didn't know that my hand was already on my gun and I shot that sucker between the eyes before he knew what hit him. I hate cops—I ridded the world of one that night. I grabbed my beer and ran out of there.

At that point John asked the young man if he knew his birth's fathers last name. When he told him it confirmed what John had suspected—it was the young man's father that he left in the other prison.

Even though the child was separated from the father and his influence. The iniquity of the father's sin was still there.

Christians today accept the fact that "I am like my dad" or "I am like my mom". But they are hoping the problem will go away. But you do not have to hope. It will go away when you realize that this is a curse and it is robbing you of your blessing.

Jesus did not get on the cross just to forgive our sins but also to break the curses off of the human race so we can be the light of the world and live in unspeakable joy.

We need to admit we still have problems and that we need a spiritual answer. There is nothing wrong (hear me) there is nothing wrong with admitting that we have a curse blocking our blessing. A curse does not mean that we are bad; a curse means that something bad is happening to us.

When we are talking about curses, we are talking about a spirit (an unclean demonic spirit). It is not to put you down; it is to give you a revelation that will set you free

Let's put this in perspective as to how all this affects you:

1. Generational curses produce a spiritual genetic code weakness toward a particular sin.
2. You are drawn to those sins like a magnet.
3. It causes you to experience failure in relationships/marriage/business, etc.
4. It causes you to believe that God doesn't love you as much as He loves others.
5. You cannot understand why some temptations are very hard for you—but they seem to be easy for others to resist.
6. It causes sin to continue through your entire family.

Now the most important question:
What Do I Do About It?

First You Must Believe:
1. Isaiah 53:5 "He was wounded for our transgressions, bruised for our iniquities the chastisement that brought our peace was upon Him." Verse 6 says; "We all like sheep have gone astray, each has turned his own way and the Lord laid on Him the iniquity of us all."

2. And you must believe that Jesus already paid the price and removed the curse. Galatians 3:13 tells us we have been redeemed from the curse of the

law (we are still under the effects of the curse but now we have a way out—His name is Jesus)

Second You Must Renounce and Repent of These Curses.
Supporting scriptures:
1. 2 Cor. 4:2 which says; *"..we have renounced secret and shameful ways."*
2. Lev. 26:40, *"If they confess their iniquity and the iniquity of their fathers. THEN I will remember My covenant.*

THE PROCESS FOR BREAKING CURSES

1. Identify the curses in your life
II. Pray the following:
    A. Renounce these curses
    B. Repent: Ask God for forgiveness of yourself.
    C. Repent: Ask God for forgiveness of your ancestor's sins on both sides of your family as far back as necessary.
    D. Forgive yourself of any and all sins.
    E. Put those sins and iniquities under the blood of Jesus (you and your ancestors sins)
    F. Close all open doors (ask God to remove any legal rights).
    G. Ask God to break any un-godly sole ties with family and others.
    H. Ask God to lift the curse from you and your descendants.

AFTER BREAKING THESE CURSES

    A. Stay in God's Word and in prayer
    B. Avoid situations where you are easily tempted
    C. Listen to praise and worship music; and
    D. Fast

Just keep yourself filled with the things and activities of God and these demonic influences caused by curses will never return.

Chapter Thirteen

THE CAUSES OF GENERATIONAL CURSES

Basically the same things that open doors for demonic invasion are also the causes of generational curses because it is the open doors of our ancestors that started these curses initially. But to clarify these open doors in a different context, let me briefly share some of the major causes.

<u>Idolatry</u>
It means to acknowledge another god before the Lord, to make a representation of it, and worship it. God punishes and judges idolatry.

<u>The Occult</u>
The occult is that which is hidden. Occult practices have always fascinated the fallen man because the three greatest aspirations of the natural man are the desire for knowledge, the longing for power, and the search for solutions to his needs.

There are two sources of power and knowledge---the power of God and the power of the enemy.

"There shall not be found among you anyone who makes his son or his daughter pass through the fire, or one who practices witchcraft, or a soothsayer, or one who conjures spells, or a medium, or a spiritist, or one who calls up the dead. For all that do these things are an abomination to the Lord, and because of these abominations the Lord your God drives them out from before you. You shall be blameless before the Lord your God."
(Deuteronomy 18:10-13)

<u>All Forms of Illicit or Unnatural Sex</u>
Homosexuality, lesbianism, sex with animals, adultery, fornication, incest, and everything illicit and illegal before the eyes of the Lord, will bring a curse." Leviticus 18:1-25

Not Honoring or Respecting Parents

There are many Sons and daughters who are not doing well in life because they do not honor and respect their parents.

"Children, obey your parents in the Lord, for this is right. Honor your father and mother, which is the first commandment with promise, that it may be well with you and you may live long on the earth." (Ephesians 6:1-3)

To Curse That Which God Has Blessed

To curse means to speak badly about something or someone. When people speak negatively about a child of God, or something that the Lord has blessed, that curse will backfire on the one who is speaking evil.

"He bows down, he lies down as a lion; and as a lion, who shall rouse him. Blessed is he who blesses you, and cursed is he who curses you." Number 24:9

"Now the Lord said to Abram: Get out of your country, from your family and from your father's house, to a land that I will show you. I will make you a great nation; I will bless you and make your name great, and you shall be a blessing. I will bless those who bless you, and curse him who curses you; and in you all families of the earth shall be blessed." Genesis 12:1-3

To Steal That Which Belongs to God

"Bring all the tithes into the storehouse, that there may be food in My house, and try Me now in this, "says the LORD of hosts, "If I will not open up for you the windows of heaven and pour out for you such blessing that there will not be enough room to receive it. And I will rebuke the devourer for your sakes, so that he will not destroy the fruit of your ground, nor shall the vine fail to bear fruit for you in the field, "says the LORD of hosts; And all nations will call you blessed, for you will be a delightful land, "says the LORD of hosts." Malachi 3:10-12

Those who do not tithe or give offerings to God sometimes ask why things are not going well with their finances. It is because a curse has come upon them for not giving God what is rightfully His.

Injustices
This especially applies when the victim is weak, widowed, orphan, impoverished or a foreigner. God will judge those who harm these people.

Generational curses are initiated by the sins of our ancestors as opposed to our own sins, and are carried down the bloodline from generation to generation. The possible effects are endless and include such things as sickness & disease, divorce, bad temper, rejection, sexual curses and much more. People often ask why they are impoverished. Why they are sick? Why is their son or daughter living a homosexual life style? Why are there so many divorces in their family? Why are their children addicted to drugs?

In life, there is always a cause and effect. Instead of looking for solutions in tree tops, we need to go to the root of the problem. Too many ministers and counselors try to solve people's problems superficially. We need to stop treating the snake bite and start killing the snake (break the curse and cast out the demon).

Chapter Fourteen

SIGNS AND INDICATIONS OF GENERATIONAL CURSES

If you experience any of the following problems, and know that they are a part of your family history, you should consider the likely possibility that it is due to a generational curse.

Mental and Emotional Disturbances
The key words here are confusion and depression.

"So you shall be driven mad because of the sight which your eyes see." Deuteronomy 28.-34

Chronic Illness
A chronic illness is one that has afflicted or killed many members of a family for generations. Doctors call these diseases genetic or hereditary. These would include such things as diabetes, high blood pressure, heart disease, asthma, cancer, and arthritis to mention just a few.

We have seen individuals with just such diseases, renounce it, break the curse, and receive deliverance, resulting in complete healing.

"The LORD will make the plague cling to you until He has consumed you from the land which you are going to possess. The LORD will strike you with consumption, with fever, with inflammation, with severe burning fever, with the sword, with scorching, and with mildew; they shall pursue you until you perish." Deuteronomy 28:21-22

Infertility
This would include the inability to conceive, a tendency to miscarry, menstrual irregularity, cysts, tumors and abortions. *"Cursed shall be the first fruit of your body and the produce of your land the increase of your cattle and the offspring of your flocks."* Deuteronomy 28:18

Disintegration of the Family
Many parents have suffered from the curse of family disintegration. They have their children dedicated to drugs and alcohol, sex, music, all forms of the occult, and end up divorced, widowed, or as unwed mothers.

Poverty or Continual Economic Insufficiency
When this curse is in operation, no matter how much money people make, they always have financial difficulty, and never see prosperity.

"Because you did not serve the Lord your God with joy and gladness of heart, for the abundance of everything, therefore you shall serve your enemies, whom the Lord will send against you, in hunger, in thirst, in nakedness, and in need of everything; and he will put a yoke of iron on your neck until He has destroyed you." Deuteronomy 28:47-48

A Sequence of Suicides, Premature or Unnatural Deaths
People afflicted by this curse frequently experience strong premonitions. We are talking about a spiritual reality, an invisible enemy who needs to be destroyed.

Self-Imposed Curses
Things we speak about ourselves.
"But I say to you that for every idle word men may speak they will give account of it in the Day of Judgment. For by your words you will be just justified and by your words you will be condemned." Matthew 12:36-37

"Death and life are in the power of the tongue. And those who love it will eat its fruit." Proverbs 18:21

There are three steps people can take to separate themselves from the bondage of negative confessions:

1. Repent for confessing bad things
2. Revoke and cancel those spoken words.
3. Replace them with the right confession

Chapter Fifteen

THE BELIEVERS AUTHORITY

Hopefully by now you understand that casting out demons, breaking curses and pulling down strongholds is not something mysterious; it is a supernatural act of God that cannot be accomplished by man alone.

As you will note in the Chapter Forty everyone has a responsibility to maintain their own deliverance, which may include self-deliverance. However, I do not recommend self-deliverance ***"initially."*** It is my opinion that a person who is under a curse or who has demonic strongholds in their life needs assistance from a trained individual who knows their spiritual authority. I am convinced a person with such significant bondage cannot free themselves, and there seems to be no scriptural evidence to the contrary.

With that said, the church needs trained deliverance ministers who know their authority over Satan and his evil army. Therefore, this section is dedicated to learning what the Bible says about the "Believer's Authority."

Introduction

"So God created man in His own image,- in the image of God He created him; male and female He created them. Then God blessed them, and God said to them; 'Be fruitful and multiply; fill the earth and subdue it, have dominion over the fish of the sea, the birds of the air, and over every living thing that moves on the earth." (Genesis 1.27-28)

The very first words God spoke to man gave us a command to multiply and then He gave man dominion (authority) over every living thing on the earth. Most importantly, He gave us authority over Satan and his demons as we see numerous times in the New Testament.

We, as believers in Jesus Christ, need to know our authority and how to use it. Too many people in the body of Christ suffer needlessly because they do not know their authority over Satan----therefore, we suffer physically, spiritually, emotionally, financially, and so on. And they also suffer because of a lack of knowledge about the gift of deliverance God provided for His church.

I am not saying you will never get sick, need money, get depressed and so forth. But I am saying, it should not be nearly as plentiful as it is in the church today. If we would exercise our faith (trust God for all things) and use our authority over Satan, our lives would be much much better.

The believer's authority has become a topic of controversy in some churches today. That is a lie of the enemy because God places a high priority on authority because He is the one who created it. The Bible says all authority comes from and originates from God. This conflict in the body of Christ comes from our failure to accept the radical difference between the authority of Jesus and the authority of the world.

The world sees authority as being grounded in law and its enforcement. It comes from the Latin word Imperium. This is the authority used by the crusaders to sack (loot, plunder and capture) the Middle East. But Jesus pointed out to His disciples that His authority is much different.

This is what Jesus told His disciple; *"You know that those who are considered rulers over the Gentiles lord it over them, and their great ones exercise authority over them. Yet, it shall not be so among you; but whoever desires to be great among you shall be your servant. And whoever of you desires to be first shall be slave to all. For even the Son of Man did not come to be served, but to serve, and give His life a ransom for many."* (Mark 10:42-45).

Jesus is telling His disciples the type of service He expects from them, and from us. The word ransom refers to Himself but it also refers to His expectations of us to serve, and give our life as a ransom for others.

The nature of the authority of Jesus can be seen in the way He used it and the authority He gave His disciples. He gave them authority and sent them out to, "Proclaim the Kingdom of God, to heal the sick, and to cast out demons." And this is the authority He has given us.

When Jesus and/or His followers healed the sick or cast out demons and led people to join the Kingdom of God and spend eternity in heaven, they were exercising their authority (1) To proclaim the gospel; and (2) their authority over Satan and his demons. They were not exercising their authority over people. That is what the world does. That is the difference in the nature of the authority used by the world and the nature of the authority given to us by Jesus.

When Jesus made disciples, He called them to follow Him so He could make them into something they were not. He called them so they could fulfill the purpose for which God created them. He freed them from bondage and sent them out to serve---to be a blessing.

When he sends us to make disciples, He sends us NOT to bring them into some bondage or into something we believe; but to meet Him and to find Him in their life.

The Meat of our Authority

"And He said to them, I saw Satan fall like lightening from heaven. Behold I give you the authority to trample on serpents and scorpions (Satan & demonic spirits) and over all the power of the enemy, and nothing shall by any means hurt you" (Luke 10:18-19)

Jesus was not referring to a vision in which He saw Satan cast out of heaven. Rather, Jesus saw Satan being defeated by the disciples (the 70 sent out). But beyond that Jesus was referring to the ultimate defeat of Satan by all His disciples—specifically the church.

Also notice that serpents and scorpions are symbols of spiritual enemies and demonic power, over which Jesus has given His follower's power.

This Scripture in Luke has to do something to you on the inside. I think it is one of the most powerful verses in the Bible. Jesus is telling us to be a warrior!! He is telling us not to worry, because He has given us authority to "squash" the enemy!!

We do not have authority over just a little bit of Satan's power, but over ALL of Satan's power. Satan has to obey us through the name of Jesus. It is time that believer's started using their authority.

There are a lot of things we can do that Satan hates. But the three most powerful, from my experience, are these: (1) Prayer (especially using your prayer language) (2) Placing the protective power of the blood of Jesus over your family daily. Satan hates this because he knows that is what defeated Him over two thousand years ago; and (3) God's Word which is the most deadly weapon we have in defeating Satan and the powers of darkness. Learn it and use it.

Tell him what scripture says and then apply the blood of Jesus. Speak it out loud—place the blood of Jesus between you and Satan.

<u>Never be frightened of or run from Satan</u>. He only has power over the believer if you give it to him.

In Luke 9:1 it says; "Jesus *called His disciples together, and gave them power and authority over all demons, and authority to heal the sick*"

This verse explains that Jesus transfers His power over demonic power (hell's works) and over human hurt of any kind to us (His disciples).

We have been given authority and power over all evil, BUT we can only expect to see spiritual breakthrough to the degree we receive and apply that authority in prayer, in preaching, in teaching, and in personal ministry to others.

As Christians we know that Satan has been defeated and we know that we have authority over him. So why do Christians still struggle and suffer at the hands of Satan?

The fact is, once you become members of God's kingdom, Satan hates you even more. He does not want to lose you nor have you bring others into salvation; so he will come against you with all his evil fury. And if you do not know your authority in Jesus you will be an easy target.

We are told in 2 Timothy 2:4 that "no one engaged in warfare entangles himself with the affairs of this life, that he may please Him who enlisted him as a soldier.

God has chosen us as soldiers in His army to come against the powers of darkness; both in our own lives and the lives of others.

Rather than entangling himself in civilian matters the soldier must dedicate himself whole heartedly to the business of being a soldier. In like manner, the warfare of the kingdom of God demand's one's full attention. We are all called to be soldiers. Therefore, if you are going to defeat Satan you must be a fighter. He has given us a complete set of armor for protection, a sword for offense, and prayer for communication.

God called His followers to be soldiers and soldiers are trained to fight. They must be disciplined, alert and obedient to the command of their captain. Likewise, the Christian is admonished to always be vigilant because the enemy is constantly seeking someone to devour. You have the authority to defeat Satan and his army of demonic spirits.

Authority to Minister to Others

Your authority as a believer goes beyond just casting out demons. You have the authority to minister to your fellow family of believers in a variety of ways.

"Most assuredly, I say to you, he who believes in Me, the works that I do he shall do also; and greater works than these will he do, because I go to My Father." John 14:12

We will discuss the works that Jesus did knowing that as Jesus was sent by the Father to speak and act on His behalf, so you as a believer know we are sent by Jesus to speak and act on His behalf.

According to Luke 4:18 believers are anointed (empowered by the Holy Spirit) to do miracles and minister to the needs of people.

"The Spirit of the Lord is upon Me, because He has anointed Me to preach the gospel to the poor; He has sent Me to heal the brokenhearted, to preach deliverance to the captives and recovery of sight to the blind, to set at liberty those who are oppressed."

Based upon this verse alone you have the authority to:

Lead People to Christ
Every believer has the authority to share the Gospel and lead people to repentance and accept Jesus Christ as Lord and Savior. Only the Holy Spirit can convict someone of their need for Him, we have the responsibility to share the message.

Baptize Them in the Holy Spirit
The Holy Spirit is what empowers the believer to be a witness. Once you have the Holy Spirit you are authorized to pray for others to be filled with the Holy Spirit (Acts 19:6)

Minister to the Brokenhearted
Whenever someone is hurt in a relationship they often experience a broken heart along with feelings of rejection, anger, bitterness and grief which often become an open door for evil spirits by those names. They also tend to build up defensive walls for protection which can open the door to additional stress and emotional pain and trauma.

A major part of Jesus' ministry was casting out demons
As a believer you also have the authority to cast evil spirits out of the brethren. This is simply doing what Jesus did and told us to do.

Heal The Sick
Sickness originates from the devil and is not God's plan for mankind. Healing the sick demonstrates the authority Jesus has given you over the powers of darkness.

Breaking Bondages
A person in bondage is someone under some external power and control....someone who is being restricted or bound. I John 4:8 tells us that Jesus came to destroy the works of the devil and since we are told to do what He did we also have the authority to break bondages and set people free.

Specific examples of bondages would include:
* Ungodly soul ties
* Word or spoken curses
* Generational curses
* Unforgiveness
* Participation in occultic activities

Blessings and Impartations
Luke 4:19 says; *"to proclaim the acceptable year of the Lord."* This verse refers to the Jewish year of Jubilee (Lev. 25). During the year of Jubilee, which happens every fifty years, debts were forgiven and people came into the blessing of their inheritance. You also have the authority to forgive:

If you forgive the sins of any, they are forgiven them; if you retain the sins of any, they are retained." (John 20:23)

You also have the authority to bless others: *And He lead them out as far as Bethany, and He lifted up His hands and blessed them."* (Luke 24:50)

To bless someone means to speak words that impart encouragement. You have the authority to impart life and the anointing of the Holy Spirit.

You also have the authority to impart into another's life. To impart means to release into someone's life the spiritual empowerment that you possess.

Chapter Sixteen

OUR SPIRITUAL ENEMY
(An Introduction to Spiritual Warfare)

Demons are spiritual enemies and it is the responsibility of every Christian to deal with them directly in spiritual warfare.

"Finally, my brethren, be strong in the Lord, and in the power of His might. Put on the whole armor of God that you may be able to stand against the wiles of the devil. For we do not wrestle against flesh and blood, but against principalities, against powers, against the rulers of the darkness of this age, against spiritual hosts of wickedness in the heavenly places." Ephesians 6:10-12

"For though we walk in the flesh, we do not war against the flesh. For the weapons of our warfare are not carnal, but mighty through God to pulling down strongholds." 2 Corinthians 10:3-4

The Apostle Paul uses the analogy of wrestling in reference to our warfare with Satan and his army of evil spirits. This is an accurate description as it speaks of up-close and personal hand-to-hand grappling with the powers of darkness. Most of us would, I am sure, prefer to blast them away with a huge cannon from as far away as possible. But this is not possible. Our battle with Satan and his army is spiritual and our weapons are spiritual. It is an in your face type of combat.

One commentary on the word "wrestle" as used in Ephesians 6:12 suggests that the actual use of this term means to "slaughter" or to "vibrate against them until you eject them."

Wrestling also suggests pressure tactics, which informs us that one of Satan's tactics is to put pressure on us. He does this in all areas of our life, including our emotions, decision making and our physical bodies.

Believers often feel pressured by the enemy in a variety of ways. Those who are unaware of his tactics try to get relief from tranquilizers, sleeping pills or the psychiatrist's couch. But God's remedy is spiritual warfare.

You cannot ignore Satan and his demons or they will defeat you. Believers must engage in warfare to be victorious.

Scripture shows how the Christian can put pressure on Satan's army and defeat them. Believers must learn the practical ways this is done. Believers must discard our fleshly weapons and take up our spiritual weapons. Believers must know and use their own weaponry, and know the tactics of the enemy if they are to live a life of victory.

Ephesians 6:12 gives us four important things about our spiritual enemy that we need to know to effectively wrestle against and defeat our enemy.

1. <u>Our battle is against PRINCIPALITIES.</u>
The Greek word for principalities is "archas." This word is used to define things in a series, such as leaders, rulers and magistrates. Therefore, a "series" of leaders or rulers would describe their rank and organization. So the word "principalities" tell us that the satanic kingdom is highly organized. Satan is the head or Commander-in-Chief of his kingdom and under him are the generals, majors, captains on down to private.

The English word for "principality" is defined as "the territory or jurisdiction of a prince or the country that gives title to a prince" (Webster). Therefore we see these ruling spirits are assigned over areas such as cities and nations. This is confirmed by the account in Daniel 10. Daniel was seeking a word from God through prayer and fasting.

After three weeks an angel appeared. The angel explained that he had been delayed in getting to Daniel with God's message by an encounter with "the prince of the kingdom of Persia."

He was not referring to an earthly prince because a mere man could not stand against a heavenly angel. Therefore, he is speaking of a demonic prince. From this it becomes clear that there are ruling demon spirits placed by Satan over nations and cities in order to carry out his evil purposes.

Problems that continually persist and plague homes and churches indicate that special evil agents have been assigned to cause trouble in these areas as well. Therefore, we discover that our spiritual warfare embraces much more than our individual lives. We are, in actuality, fighting for the welfare of our homes, our communities and our nation.

The enemy is thoroughly organized and his moves are made with evil design to steal, kill and destroy

2. Our warfare is against POWERS
The Greek word translated powers is "exousias". The most accurate translation is "authorities."

This word tells us that the demons that are placed over certain areas or territories are given authority to carry out whatever orders they have been assigned. As Christian soldiers we are not to be dismayed or discouraged to learn that those whom we wrestle against have been given authority, because as believers we have even greater authority. All true Christians are vested with the authority in the name of Jesus.

"And these signs will follow them who believe: IN MY NAME they shall cast out demons." (Mark 16:17) This verse tells us that we, as believers, have greater authority than the authority of demons. Demons are forced to yield to the authority of the name of Jesus.

Scripture also tells us that demons not only have authority but they also have power. In Luke 10:19 we read of the power of the enemy. The word "power" in the Greek is *"dunamis."* Our English words dynamo and dynamite come from this word. Yet this fact should not worry the Christian soldier, because he has the promise of God's Word that he can overcome the devil.

"But you shall receive power, after the Holy Spirit has come   upon you."
Acts 1:8

The power of the believer comes to him with the baptism of the Holy Spirit. Jesus knows His followers need both authority and power to deal with the enemy. When Jesus sent out the twelve to ministry He sent them fully equipped.

"Then He called His twelve disciples together, and gave them POWER (dunamis) and AUTHORITY (exousia) over all devils, and to cure diseases." Luke 9:1

The same was true when He sent out the seventy as recorded in Luke 10:17-19.

The commission that Jesus has given His church provides the same authority and power as stated in Mark 16:17. This promise was not limited to the apostles or first century disciples, but it is for all believers of all times.

The commission we are given in Matthew 28:18-20, opens with the declaration, "all power (authority) is given unto Me in heaven and earth. Go therefore. ..."

Today, we have the same power and authority for ministry that was given to the church initially. We just need to believe it. It would literally be nonsense, not to mention dangerous, to stand against demon spirits without this power and authority. This authority comes through salvation; the power comes through the baptism in the Holy Spirit.

The evidence that the power comes through the baptism in the Holy Spirit is found in two places in scripture: (1) Acts 1:8 which says; *"But you shall receive power when the Holy Spirit has come upon you..."* and (2)1Corinthians 12:7-11 which declares the operation of the gifts of the Spirit. The gifts of the Spirit, such as supernatural words of knowledge and discerning of spirits, are indispensable in spiritual warfare.

A Christian would be foolish to go against demon forces without both his authority and power. . .both his salvation and baptism in the Holy Spirit.

Too many Christians are waiting for God to come to their rescue. Don't waste time praying that God will provide you the power and authority to overcome Satan. He has already provided it through our salvation and the baptism in the Holy Spirit. Therefore, He is waiting for us to recognize that He has already made the necessary provisions, and that we are to engage in spiritual warfare and become the militant church prophesied in Matthew 16:18; *"And I also say to you, that you are Peter, and on this rock I will build My church, and the gates of hell shall not prevail against it"*

3. We wrestle against THE RULERS OF DARKNESS OF THIS WORLD.

The word in Greek for "world rulers" is "kosmokratoras. This word is translated as "lords of the world" or "princes of this age." This shows us that the enemies intention is to control. Satan is referred to in scripture as *"the god of this world"* (2 Corinthians 4:4).

When Adam fell through sin, Satan gained dominion over the world. Jesus did not deny the devil's claim made during the wilderness temptations.

"Again the devil took Him up on an exceedingly high mountain, and showed Him all the kingdoms of the world and their glory. And he (Satan) said to Him, all these things I will give You, if you fall down and worship me." (Matthew 4:8-9)

It is true that Satan has dominion over the earth. But it is imperative for the believer to recognize that Satan is a defeated foe and we have every right to treat him as a trespasser.

Granted, Satan is still trying to rule the world, and he has made considerable progress. But the reason is because the church has not risen up in the power and authority we have been given. We keep waiting for Him to show up and do it for us. But He has done all He needs to do, it is now up to us.

There is however, a larger portion of the body of Christ today coming into the knowledge of the enemy and the weaponry that God has provided. And the more Christians who enter the fight, the more Satan will suffer the loss.

4. We wrestle against SPIRITUAL WICKEDNESS IN HIGH PLACES

The key here is the word wickedness. This word suggests something that is greatly destructive in nature.

These evil powers have only one objective: wickedness! They may appear as angles of light but it is a deception to draw you into their nets of destruction. Jesus exposed their evil purposes when He said: *"The thief does not come expect to steal, and kill, and to destroy..."* John 10:10a

These four descriptions found in Ephesians 6:12 give us a very vivid picture of Satan's kingdom. It is highly organized. Demon powers are placed in strategic places and given authority by Satan to control the entire world and plague it with wickedness. There is no advantage to us ignoring Satan's army or his methods because it only permits him to work undetected and unchallenged.

To fail to become actively involved in spiritual warfare is to suggest that we do not care what becomes of ourselves, our loved ones, our community, our nation and our world.

Most Christians have not become engaged in spiritual warfare because they have never been taught the importance of it nor the way to go about it. But Satan is flaunting his power through spiritism, occultism, false religions, cults, personal attacks on the minds, emotions and physical bodies of believers, like never before in human history. It is time that churches begin to identify and utilize its own power and authority.

Billy Graham was once quoted by a national newspaper as saying, "All of us engaged in Christian work are constantly aware of the fact that we have to do battle with supernatural forces and powers. . . It is perfectly obvious to all of us in spiritual work that people can be possessed by demons, harassed by them and controlled by them. More and more ministers will have to learn to use the power of God to release people from these terrible possessions by the devil."

In recent years God has been raising up a mighty army to go forth in spiritual warfare using the weapons He has provided. The results to date are impressive as thousands of God's people are being set free from the torments of demon spirits. But we have only reached the tip of the iceberg. Therefore, God is again recruiting warriors to engage the enemy in spiritual warfare and for some to enter the ministry of deliverance. Therefore, the following chapter will discuss the topic of spiritual warfare in greater detail.

Chapter Seventeen

SPIRITUAL WARFARE

What is spiritual warfare? Spiritual warfare is a matter of fighting back--getting tired of being beat up all the time by our enemy the devil.

If a thief comes to your house to steal, kill and destroy are you going to let him in and just lay down and die? I don't think so! Then why do you allow our spiritual enemy to do it to you?

The Body of Christ is just too darn passive. If your child was being bullied on the playground—pushed off the swing; knocked off the titter totter, knocked down and called names—what would you do? Nothing? No, you would step in and make it stop.

Why are we in the church so passive in the spiritual realm? We allow the devil to hurt and torment ourselves, our children, our spouse, our friends and we passively stand by and do nothing. Who are we afraid of? The Bible says that; *"He who lives in us is greater than he who is in the world."* If you believe that then fear wouldn't be a problem.

Everyone has (and needs) a purpose in life—a God given task to accomplish during our life here on earth. And we all have one. On the other hand, we have an enemy called the devil who also has a purpose: it is to destroy both you and your ministry. But you have the power to prevent him from doing that. We call it the prayers of a warrior or spiritual warfare.

We need to utilize spiritual warfare prayers daily because the devil attacks daily. Let me put this another way: You don't want to put a fence up and lock the door after the theft comes in—you do these things before he comes. So start your day by defeating your enemy before he has time to fulfill his purpose, which is to kill, steal and destroy. You can either let him get away with it or you can stop him—it's your choice.

Your true identity is not what you do for a living, or who you are married to, the size house you live in, or who your children are. Your identity is what

God has promised in your life—your Godly purpose. Don't let the devil steal your identity.

Before we begin to discuss what spiritual warfare is and how we are to operate in it, let me first share a little something about preparing for Spiritual Warfare.

We all know that: *Victory begins with the name of Jesus on our lips. But it is consummated by the nature of Jesus in our heart.* Therefore, it is important that you remember <u>that the major objective of spiritual warfare, as is the purpose of worship, deliverance and every spiritual thing we do, is to become Christ-like.</u>

<u>So How Are We to Prepare For Spiritual Battle?</u>
The very first thing we do is put on the armor of God as explained in Ephesians 6. Each is of great importance but there is one you can never forget. You can have a warm heart that is full of the love of Jesus and it can be protected by the breastplate of righteousness. You can gird yourself with the truth, shod your feet with the gospel of peace, carry a shield by living in faith knowing and trusting God's Word, and you can know God's Word thereby, carrying the sword of God's Spirit. However, too often we never put on the helmet of salvation. We think we are saved and therefore we are okay. The reason being: Our major battle ground is our mind. This is where Satan sets up a stronghold—What is a stronghold of the mind? It is a demonically induced pattern of thinking.

The Christian needs to protect himself and break that pattern of thinking. For example, when thoughts of worry, fear, anger, hatred, etc. come to mind what do you do? Do you entertain them, dwell on them and let that emotion get the best of you; or do you rebuke it immediately and began to trust God for the circumstance?

Anytime these negative thoughts of anger, fear, worry, hatred, etc. remain, it either is, or will become, a stronghold. And remember Prov. 23:7 says, *"As a man thinks in his heart, so he is."* What does this mean specifically? It means this; the essence of who we are is in our thought life.

Every time you get a thought if you will just pause for a moment you will know if that thought is from God or the enemy, and then you have a choice. Accept it or reject it.

You can continue with a negative thought, or you can put it under the blood of Jesus and tell the devil to take a hike. But if you find this nearly impossible to do then stop pretending everything is "all right." Humble yourself and get some help through a proven deliverance ministry. I say humble because you must be willing to admit you need deliverance or you will never be free from strongholds.

Spiritual warfare is a necessity for every believer because it will do several things for you: It will help protect you; minimize and/or shorten the enemies attacks; it will provide ultimate victory; it will help remove the road blocks Satan uses to stop your assigned ministry from God; and combined with deliverance it will set you free from the yokes of bondage and influence of unclean spirits. Spiritual warfare is important.

There has been a great deal written about Spiritual Warfare and if you been a follower of Jesus for very long you have probably heard this term tossed around a lot, and even debated by those who vary in their doctrine. I will grant you that such debate has led to confusion for some. Also there has been a lack of teaching on this subject. The combination of these two things (confusion & lack of teaching which in turn brings a lack of understanding) has caused many believers to completely avoid spiritual warfare.

The objective in this chapter is to try and present an understandable overview of spiritual warfare. The purpose is to assist you in learning how to defeat Satan and his army of demons; and thereby help you become the spiritual warrior God desires you to be.

First, of course, you must put on the armor of God. And how do we do that? We verbally place it on our bodies and then we live it!

NOTE: *For detailed information on the Armor of God see Appendix Three. It includes a description of each piece of armor along with its Practical*

Military Purpose and its *Spiritual Warfare Application.*

But, in addition to putting on the armor of God; I believe there are two major components to spiritual warfare:

First is Prayer: Not just any prayer but specific prayers against the devil and his tactics, as well as removing the legal rights he has in your life. It is a spiritual in your face confrontation with the devil. Some people fear this but if you ignore him, as so many in the church do today, he won't go away. Rather, you simply become an easy target. Christians need to realize that Jesus already won the battle so you start your fight knowing you will win.

Second is: Knowing and using your authority in Jesus name. Our enemy is an ancient, very crafty and treacherous foe. He also doesn't play by any rules of fairness. And as we learned previously, our sins and the sins of our ancestors are open doors for Satan's demonic army to enter and torment us. But our only villain isn't sin, it is ignorance.

Just like most believers are unaware of the availability and blessings of deliverance, most Christians are ignorant about spiritual warfare. In fact, few know what it truly is. Yet it is the first, and most important, step in defeating Satan and his gang of cut-throat demons.

Don't get me wrong, I know a lot of Christians who can pray anointed prayers. But few really engage in spiritual warfare. In fact, the introduction of spiritual warfare often is critical if we are to defeat our enemy. But when we move from knowing what it is to understanding what it is, most people are more willing to participate.

Satan's objective is to utilize his followers (demons) to defeat and hurt you on a daily basis. Our responsibility as Christians must be to meet him head on with the power and authority we have been given and thereby, defeating the attacks of Satan and those demons assigned to us.

How is that accomplished? From my personal experience, which has been to follow the example of Jesus, my advice is to get up early and beat him up first. Just like in any battle or fight, it is always best to throw the first punch.

Learn to pray with authority and your first blow may knock him out for the entire day. I get up at 4:00 A.M. every morning to do just that. You don't have to get up that early but get up early enough to spend 30 minutes to an hour with Him and in spiritual warfare and I promise you daily circumstances will improve.

So how does one get trained in spiritual warfare? Well, if you are familiar with the life of King David it will take very little effort to figure out how he became a skillful spiritual warrior. As David is our example, the best way to be trained to be a skillful warrior is to be taught what it is and then be placed in the heat of battle.

It is only when you are placed in the furnace of affliction, when it seems the earth opens up and all hell begins to break loose in your life that you can truly be trained in the art of strategic prayer and spiritual warfare.

It is only when God trains you in the midst of an actual battle that you can gain true experience. Simply reading the Bible or attending workshops and conferences will never make you an effective warrior. These are great places to learn about spiritual warfare but it is the battle itself where you get trained because this is where you experience the power, authority and victory available to all believers who are willing to participate in prayer warfare. And each time you engage the enemy you become stronger and obtain greater faith.

It is only when God places you in the middle of a battle or an impossible situation when there is no one or nothing that can save or deliver you but God, that a true spiritual warrior can be born. And being a strong warrior is the only way you will ever minimize your attacks and truly defeat the enemy.

Are you aware of someone who at one time was on fire for God but today they are nowhere to be found in the Christian community? Sure, we all do. Why did this happen? Probably because the battle (attacks, struggle and afflictions) became more than they could handle and they found it easier to go back to their old way of life.

More than likely they did not understand and/or utilize spiritual warfare. But before you ever consider giving up, giving in, or falling prey to the strategies of the enemy, consider your times of struggle, testing and temptation as divine opportunities to be trained in the art of strategic prayer and spiritual warfare. Opportunities? That's right. You can be assured that these times are training sessions that God has selected to bring you into true dominion. I am not saying it is easy, but it is necessary.

The Bible states that believers should *"pray and not faint. . .least Satan should get an advantage of us; for we are not ignorant of his devices"* (Luke 18:1; II Cor. 2:11). Satan is always planning and plotting your demise. Don't let him get away with it. You must begin to war for your purpose and destiny by effectively using the Word of God. We must remain strong and defeat our enemy, not just win a few battles.

Most believers today are satisfied with a victory here and there: a healing, a financial blessing, a prophetic word, or whatever---but they never experience the full victory that God intends for them to have. Yet it is available to every believer.

So how do we obtain this victory in every aspect of our life—It is called "Spiritual Warfare". What is spiritual warfare? It is facing the enemy and his demons face to face in battle, which is an unsettling concept for many in God's house today. But it shouldn't be.

I know firsthand how nasty the devil can be. He doesn't like our ministry and he has on more than one occasion tried to destroy us and the ministry. But each time we get stronger and we better understand our authority.

All that is needed is to pray specific prayers against evil and then, when it is necessary, take your authority over Satan and his demons and expel them from your life and the lives of others---It is called deliverance or as Jesus said; "casting out demons."

Let me repeat:
Scripture makes it clear that we are soldiers in God's army, and soldiers are

expected to fight. If we fail to do so than Satan gains the advantage.

The enemy would love to create shipwrecks out of your life, your ministry, your family, and your relationships. But you must learn to effectively use the Word of God to counter act every attack. That's what Jesus did in the wilderness.

The Bible is a conglomerate of prophecies and promises that you can use as weapons against the enemy. Here's one of the keys to spiritual warfare: Pray the promise instead of the problem. Instead of praying your worries, pray the Word.

Scripture tells us that it is the power of the spoken word that gives you life or death and releases blessings or curses (Prob.18:21). You must use these words, God's Word to be specific, to destroy the works of the enemy in your life, home, ministry, community and ultimately the world. Your prayers, according to Rev. 5:8, are the incense that fills the golden bowls in heaven

Replace all ineffective words with anointed words. Spiritual warfare prayers have the ability to destroy yokes of bondage; burdens can be lifted, your life and the lives of loved ones can be revolutionized, your ministry energized, and enemy horrified. It is all a matter of praying God's promises and prophecies.

I am not talking just about intercessors. I do believe that God, in these last days, is raising anointed intercessors (anointed prayer warriors) to battle the powers of darkness over communities, governments, corporations, countries, kingdoms and nations to bring them into divine alignment. If you are one of those people you have been given a blessed task.

But I am talking to every believer in Jesus Christ. Because we are all called to spiritual warfare.

Let me share another key point about praying spiritual warfare prayers. The Bible tells us there is power in numbers. It clearly states that if two touch and agree on anything that is asked, "it shall be done" and that "one can chase a thousand, and two can put ten thousand to flight" (I Cor. 18:19; Deut. 32:30).

Praying with others increases your power base. So, pray with your spouse or a prayer partner or a small prayer group. But only those that desire to focus on spiritual warfare (praying specific prayers against the enemy).

In Chapter 15 we spoke about the importance of knowing your authority. Just like with deliverance, to wage effective spiritual warfare, we must understand our authority. And our authority and victory over every circumstance, comes when we begin refusing to judge what we see and what we hear, and begin trusting what God has promised will come to pass.

We will never know Christ's victory to its fullest until we stop reacting humanly to our circumstances. Listen; when you truly have victory over something you can look at that thing without worry, fear or anxiety. This state of being is called peace. God desires that you experience this peace in your life. This peace is the proof of your victory.

Jesus first defeated Satan in the wilderness using the Word. Then He used His authority over His circumstances. This is spiritual warfare. When Jesus faced the violent storms recorded in Matt. 8:23-27, He didn't have to fight against the storm, nor did He fear it. He faced it with authority and He did it in perfect peace.

This is what God wants us to do. Pray anointed prayers by using the Word against the enemy being specific to every circumstance you pray about, as Jesus did in His wilderness experience. Then face the enemy everyday with confidence in your authority which brings peace to your circumstances and ultimately it will bring victory.

Satan's weapons are things like worry, doubt, fear, self-pity and so on (mind strongholds). Every one of these weapons robs you of peace and leaves you troubled on the inside. When it comes to any relationship (with Satan or another human) whenever there is not peace, there is war.

Peace is Spirit Power: And when you engage in spiritual warfare and use your spiritual authority you will experience spiritual peace and power. A peacemaker is not merely someone who protests against war, he is actually someone who is inwardly so yielded to Christ in spirit and purpose that he can truly be called a "son of God." Where he goes, God goes and where God goes, he goes. He is fearless, bold and calm. Peace and power emanates from him the way heat radiates from a fire. This is available to every believer who engages in spiritual warfare.

We also know that Satan attacks our physical body as well as our mind and emotions. So the whole armor of God is needed. But you can deal with the physical attacks as you do the mind attacks—you engage in battle through prayer and you cast out whatever is causing the illness or disease... followed by prayers of healing.

You may be thinking; "this sounds great but I don't know where to begin". Not to worry-just relax, I will deal with, and end with, that question in just a few minutes. But first let me encourage you with this:

Often times God moves you into a dimension where you go through a period of time that causes you to wonder if the Lord is against you. It's almost as if God somehow becomes "different" from the One you've learned to trust and rely on. He seems quite, distant, maybe uncaring or unconcerned at times. We have all experienced such times. This also seems to be the relationship God has had with His church the past few years.

Time to worry? Absolutely not! Sometimes, individuals and the church as a whole, feel like the Lord is pulling them through a knot hole backwards-- like God has His sword drawn and the tip is aimed straight at your heart. Almost like God is against you.

Let me assure you that God is not against you, He is for you. In fact, it is His express purpose to release this same sword of the spirit, which is the Word of God, through your words and prayers.

But before the Lord's will comes through your mouth, it must first pass through your heart. This is not something to fear, it is God getting you ready for battle because God's purpose is to make you a spiritual warrior.

How do you begin the process of learning spiritual warfare? The very best way to begin—is to use sample warfare prayers prepared by those who already use the anointed Word of God to decree and declare their freedom, nullify the enemy's attacks and claim victory in Jesus Name. You can always adjust them to meet your specific circumstances. I have included a sample warfare prayer at the end of this chapter.

In addition to learning how to pray such prayers, be willing to submit to God's mechanism for setting you free from yokes of bondage and tormenting spirits. Find a trusted deliverance ministry and get set free.

I realize that this is not a surprise to anyone but we are in the last days before Jesus comes for His church. And if you have noticed, in scripture God always saves the best to last—the latter is always better then the former.

Think about that—because you are part of the last days—you are the latter and not the former. He saved His best to last. He saved you for such a time as this. You need to get about God's business. Isn't it time we returned to our first love?

Isn't it time we begin to share the gospel with someone--every day? Isn't it time we get set free and begin to set others free of demonic influence and sin? Isn't it time we begin to defeat Satan at every turn by casting down the strongholds of our minds? And isn't it time we begin warring in the spirit and defeating Satan on a consistent basis in our life, the lives of family and friends, and the lives of our brothers and sisters in Christ? Isn't it time?

SAMPLE WARFARE PRAYER
(A Powerful Daily Prayer)

As your servant, Oh God, I confess my continued allegiance and surrender myself completely in every area of my life. I cover myself and my family with the blood of Jesus for our protection. I take a stand against all the workings of Satan and his demons that would hinder me or any family member.

I place upon myself, with thanksgiving, the Armor You have provided: The Girdle of Truth, The Breastplate of Righteousness, The Sandals of Peace, The Shield of Faith, and The Helmet of Salvation. And I take up The Sword of the Spirit.

By faith and dependence upon You I put off all fleshly works of the old man and stand in the victory of the cross where Jesus provided cleansing from the old man and has provided a way for me to live above sin.

Heavenly Father, I give You thanks that I am seated in the heavenlies, and I recognize by faith that all wicked (demonic) spirits and Satan himself are under my feet and are subject to me in the name of Jesus.

Father, I thank You that the weapons of our warfare are not carnal but mighty through God for pulling down strongholds, to casting down imaginations and every high thing that exalts itself against the knowledge of God, and to bring every thought into obedience to the Lord Jesus Christ.

Therefore, in my own life today, I will tear down the strongholds of Satan and smash his plans that have been formed against me.

I tear down the strongholds of Satan against my mind, and I surrender my mind to the Holy Spirit. I affirm that my Heavenly Father did not give me a spirit of fear, but a spirit of power, of love and a sound mind.

I break and smash the strongholds of Satan formed against my emotions today and I give my emotions to You. I smash the strongholds of Satan formed against my will today. I give my will to You, and choose to make the right decisions of faith and obedience.

I smash the strongholds of Satan formed against my body today, and I declare that no disease, bacteria, virus or illness of any kind can live on or in this body. I give my body to You Father recognizing that I am Your temple. I rejoice in Your mercy and goodness.

I decree and declare:

- All works of the enemy that are contrary to or would hinder the fulfillment of God's plan and purpose in my life are broken.

- I am liberated from all generational, spoken or satanic curses. I sever them by the sword (Word of God), the Spirit and the blood.

- I am free from any and all demonic influences that negatively affect me physically, emotionally, psychologically, spiritually or by any other means.

- Neither Satan nor his fallen angels have any right to my finances and that all the wealth of the wicked comes to me now.

- Satan cannot cause confusion nor interfere with my hearing the voice of God regarding my daily ministry assignment.

- The wisdom of God directs my life and cannot be twisted or perverted in any way.

- I will stand in victory against all attacks of the enemy and will destroy all attempts to deceive me, to ambush me or to interfere with my assigned ministry.

- Through prayer, worship and obedience to God I will continue to defeat Satan and his unclean spirits.

In the name of Jesus I repent of, bind up, rebuke, cast out, nullify, and forbid off myself, my wife/husband, my family, my friends, my church, and my community the following demonic spirits:

Spirit of poverty; religious and pharisaical spirits; mindsets of lack, worry &fear; spirits of witchcraft and control; selfishness; spirits of lust & sexual immorality; pride; fear & timidity; self-righteousness; spirits of apathy & lukewarmness; negative thoughts & ideas; rebellion; depression; compromise with the world; intimidation; discouragement; accusation; self-gratification; spirits of death & suicide; and all spirits associated with mental, emotional or physical illness.

I pull down every generational curse, all hexes and word curses. I call all my relationships into Godly order. I decree and declare my life is under and in the order of God Almighty.

I pray that now and through this day You would strengthen and enlighten me, show me Father the ways Satan is hindering and tempting and lying and distorting the truth in my life. Enable me to be aggressive mentally, to think about and practice Your Word, and give You Your rightful place in my life.

I pray that the Holy Spirit would bring all the work of the crucifixion, all the work of the resurrection, all the work of the glorification, and all the work of Pentecost into my life today.

In Jesus name this life You have given me, is Yours completely. My God is Jehovah and He is the God who saves, heals and delivers. Therefore, I refuse to be discouraged, to worry or to speak negatively. You are the God of hope. Teach me to speak blessings and not curses.

You have proven Your power by resurrecting Jesus from the dead, and I claim in every way this power and victory over all satanic forces in my life.

I pray this pray in the name of the Lord Jesus Christ with thanksgiving. I seal this prayer by the blood of the Lamb.   Amen.

Chapter Eighteen

LEGAL RIGHTS AND RECLAIMING LEGAL GROUND

A major part of any deliverance includes removing legal rights. If you try to cast out demons without first removing its legal right to be there, then you cannot expect to achieve a complete or successful deliverance.

Do you ever feel like the devil has a key to your front door? He walks in, does whatever he wants, and won't leave, even when you try and throw him out. If so, then it is time to take away his keys.

The first step is to determine how Satan gained entrance into your life. In spiritual terms this is called "legal ground." Legal ground occurs when Satan has a right to be in your life because you or someone else in authority—your parents or someone in your ancestral line—have shaken hands with the enemy and welcomed him in.

Even if you are seeking to live in obedience to the Lord, you may be paying the price for bad decisions made by your parents or your ancestors. A successful deliverance is dependent upon removing any and all legal rights.

What is a Legal Right?
A legal right is something that can give demons an opportunity to enter or harass us, or give them the right to remain in us even when we try to cast them out. Some of the most common legal rights we have discovered while ministering deliverance are:

1. **Sins**
2. **Soul Ties**
3. **Demonic Vows**
4. **Unforgiveness**
5. **Generational Curses**
6. **Childhood Rejections**
7. **Spoken Curses**
8. **Cursed Objects**

The Bible tells us not to "give place to the devil" (Ephesians 4:27). The word "place" in the Greek is the word *"topos,"* which means a literal place or terrain. You are not to give Satan any terrain in your life. He cannot come in whenever he decides, unless you have given him that right. If he does come in, it means you have given him legal ground.

As we have already learned many Christians give him access and hand him the Keys to the front door of their lives in a variety of ways without even realizing what they are doing. For example palm reading, studying astrology, reading tarot cards or horoscopes. Also watching horror movies and certain television shows, or reading certain books can be an open door. Sin, pornography, addictions, etc... will also open doors and give Satan legal ground.

Any time you give Satan legal ground it is like me going to a judge and obtaining a legal document that gives me the right to enter your home anytime I want, day or night. BUT, as a home owner you can get the judge to rescind that order.

Reclaiming Lost Ground: After Satan has devised a method by which he gains access into our lives legally, he cannot be removed until this "legal ground" is recovered. <u>Legal ground can only be recovered through breaking curses & soul ties and through genuine repentance</u> (personal repentance or asking for repentance for our ancestors who sinned). Many believers feel sorry after they sin, but are unwilling to turn from their sin. True repentance means feeling such regret over our past action or attitude that we change our mind and our action. We turn from sin and towards God and actually have a hatred for the sin we committed.

God is not in the quick-fix business. Neither repentance nor deliverance is a quick-fix. You still have to walk in your gained freedom. That is, live a life obedient to God's Word.

God has already destroyed Satan's legal right to our lives on the cross. When we choose to fellowship with darkness rather than light, we are choosing bondage rather than freedom. But when you willingly repent in your heart and turn away from your sin, what is legally yours becomes experientially yours.

The deliverance ministry team must make every attempt to know the persons heart who desires deliverance. We have learned to ask people if they are truly willing to repent of, and turn away from, a specific lifestyle (i.e. homosexuality, adultery, a specific addiction, sexual immorality).

If they are not, deliverance and praying for healing would be a waste of time. On occasion we have someone say yes and then they went right back into their sin that opened the door in the first place. So now we actually explain repentance. That it means you must hate the sin that has enslaved you. You must be sick of it, tired of serving it and willing to turn away from doing it. **True or genuine repentance will change your outward behavior!!!!**

We make people call it what it is, what God calls it: ***SIN.*** So often we want to give it a socially accepted name like "sickness" or "disease." But when demonic forces take hold and bring you to the point of addiction, it is not merely a sickness or disease. It is bondage brought on by the enemy.

Freedom will never come until you repent and let God take away the enemy's legal ground. But when you do, our Father delights in showing mercy and the Holy Spirit rushes to our aid.

When people are willing to truly repent, demons have no power to stand in the presence of the Lord Jesus Christ. *"If we confess our sin, He is faithful and just to forgive us our sins, and cleanse us from all unrighteousness."* I John 1:9

Chapter Nineteen

SOUL TIES

The purpose of this chapter about soul ties is to answer the many questions typically associated with this topic. Specifically: What are soul ties? What is the scriptural basis for understanding soul ties? How are they formed? Are they always demonic? What danger is there in soul ties? And how can they be broken?

There are times when we experience spiritual truth before we understand it. As you may recall, the one hundred and twenty in the upper room who received the baptism in the Holy Spirit on the day of Pentecost, received it before they understood it.

My wife and I dealt with soul ties in the initial years of our deliverance ministry prior to understanding them. Back then we heard them called "unholy alliances" or "perverse relationships." However, we learned early on that these "alliances" or "soul ties" were present and their power needed to be broken in individuals lives.

Good Soul Ties
Soul ties are formed when two or more persons become bonded together. Some soul ties are good, and others are evil; some are holy and some are ungodly. God has ordained and sanctioned the soul ties of bonding between children and parents, husbands and wives, friends with friends, and Christians with one another as members of the Body of Christ.

Good soul ties are founded upon the law of love, which the bible calls "the law of Christ" in Galatians 6:2, and "the royal law" in James 2:8. Therefore, the soul ties approved by God represent the bonding of people together in agape love.

For the person not familiar with soul ties related to these topics I encourage you to read and the following scriptures:

1. Ties of Marriage: Ephesians 5:22-32
2. Ties to Friendship: Jonathan was knit to the soul of David (I Sam. 18:1). Also read Proverbs 17:17 and 18:24
3. Ties of Parent/Child: Genesis 44:20, 30 (Amplified)

Demonic Soul Ties

Demonic soul ties are perversions of the good and holy soul ties. Good soul ties are founded upon love; demonic soul ties are founded upon lust. Remember that Satan cannot go beyond his limited rights; he must work within the framework of what he is allowed.. Therefore, when he gets the opportunity, he will pervert that which is pure.

When you understand soul ties you will understand that people not only need to be delivered from demons but also from other people. Ungodly soul ties are avenues through which spirits of control, domination, witchcraft and manipulation operate. I you are linked (bonded) with the wrong people, you will be in bondage, often without even knowing it.

It is never the will of God for one individual to control another. True deliverance is being delivered from any controlling power that hinders you from fulfilling the will of God.

An ungodly soul tie will result in the presence of an evil influence in your life. While good soul ties help you walk with God, ungodly soul ties hinder you in your walk with the Lord.

Ungodly soul ties in the Bible include: Ahab and Jezebel (I Kings 18); Solomon and his wives--they turned the heart of the people away from God (I Kings 11:1-4); and Levi and Simeon (Gen. 49:5-7).

When there is an unequal yoke between a believer and an unbeliever, this is also called an ungodly soul tie.

Soul ties are invisible bands or yokes in the spiritual realm; and they are either sexual or emotional. Sexual soul ties are developed whenever two people have a sexual relation outside of wedlock. Emotional soul ties are developed through co-dependency (inordinate affection) with another person.

The person who is controlling and manipulating the other person based upon emotional dependency always suffers from rejection and insecurity and try to cover it up through manipulation and control. Often times they will bully the other person through guilt and shame.

Ties Formed Through Fornication

"...do you not know that he who is joined to a harlot is one body with her? For the two, He says, shall become one flesh."

Through sexual relationships outside of marriage, demonic soul ties are formed. Those who engage in sex outside of marriage, become the one flesh which God planned solely for a husband and wife.

Through adultery, an evil soul tie is created in lust, and this demonic soul tie can destroy the holy union of marriage which is based upon mutual love and trust. When love and trust are betrayed through adultery, it is very difficult (although not impossible) to restore the shattered bonds of marital oneness. Even through "inappropriate touching" or "petting" outside of marriage, passions are aroused and demonic soul ties are created.

Excessive physical touching outside of marriage leads to the formation of a soul tie of lust, which is an open door to that very demonic spirit.

Perverse soul ties are not limited to those formed between persons of the opposite sex; they are also formed between those of the same sex through sodomy. Homosexuals, both gays and lesbians, attempt to remove the stigma of their sin by referring to themselves as "lovers," but the Word of God
declares that their motivation is lust:

"For even their women exchanged the natural use for what is against nature. Likewise also the men, leaving the natural use of a women, burned in their lust for one another, men with men committing what is shameful, and receiving in themselves the penalty of their error which was due."
(Rom.1:26-27)

In addition, perverse soul ties include those formed between men and animals. The ultimate expression of this type of sexuality is bestiality: lying carnally with animals. Some soul ties with animals fall short of bestiality and are characterized by false compassion and inordinate affection for animals.

Ties With Evil Companions
"Do not be deceived, bad (evil) company corrupts good character." I Cor. 15:33 (NIV).

Bad, or evil, company is referring to companions, associations and friendships. A person is greatly influenced by his friends, so it is important to choose righteous and holy friends. This is, of course, one reason for not associating with the unsaved.

Scripture also tells us to *"have no fellowship with the unfruitful works of darkness, but rather expose them."* (Ephesians 5:11).

We are not told here to shun unbelievers but that we are not to partake of the ungodly deeds of others. Then in verses 12 and 13 of Ephesians 5, we are given a simple way to determine whether or not our contact with the lost is godly or not. Scripture tells us we are to reprove their actions; we are to expose their sin.

If we can do that then we are probably relating to them in a proper way. BUT, if we are not exposing their deeds to the light of Christ, we should question whether our relationship with them is God's will. Why would God want you to associate with an unsaved person if you aren't exposing their sin and sharing the light of Christ?

The word expose is self-explanatory. It means to "rebuke," "reprove," "tell him his fault or sin." Then we are to convince them they are wrong. The fact of scripture is this: We are to take a stand against ungodliness and those involved in acts of darkness. If we are not doing that then we should not be in fellowship with them.

Ephesians 5:13 says, *"...all things that are exposed are made manifest by the light, for whatever makes manifest is light."*

This verse discounts the misunderstood and wrongly taught idea that living a godly life is the only witness we need. It is a deception of the enemy to think our lives alone will shed God's light on the darkness of the world. It is true that speech without a godly life is hypocritical and often turns people away from the truth. BUT a godly lifestyle without openly expressing the source of our godliness only brings glory to ourselves---rather than God. We are instructed to verbally express our witness.

Soul ties with evil companions will ensnare you, and you will find yourself entangled in wickedness. *"Thorns and snares are in the way of the perverse; He who guards his soul will be far from them... ...Make no friendship with an angry man ...least you learn his ways and set a snare for your soul."* (Proverbs 22: 5, 24, 25)

<u>Perverted Family Ties</u>

Within a family, there are close soul ties, any of which Satan is eager to pervert. The soul ties between a parent and a child can be healthy and beneficial, except when it continues into the adult life of a child.

The familiar expression, "cutting the apron strings," actually speaks of severing the soul tie between the parent and the offspring. When a son or daughter is ready for marriage, the soul tie with the parents must be terminated in order for the soul tie between husband and wife to be formed. God decrees, *"A man shall leave his father and mother and be joined to his wife"* (Eph. 5:3 1).

When a father gives his daughter in marriage, he severs the soul tie with her in consideration of her husband. When the soul tie between child and parent is not severed, then that which was good and beneficial becomes evil through control and possessiveness.

Leaving one's father and mother is not breaking relationship with them. Rather, it is actually maturing the child/parent relationship. A child must never stop honoring his father and mother, but the soul tie must be severed.

Sexual perversion within family relationships has become alarmingly prevalent. A minimum of 85% of women to whom we minister deliverance, and at least 60% of the men, have been sexually abused by a family member. This perversion occurs when there is an incestuous copulation (fancy word for intercourse) between father and daughter, mother and son, brother and sister, father-in-law and daughter-in-law, mother-in-law and son-in-law, uncles, aunts, cousins or any other close relative.

Soul Ties With The Dead
When a family member or close friend dies, the soul tie formed with that person must be dissolved. The period of sorrow, following the death of a loved one, is a time of adjustment during which the soul tie ended, yet the fond and loving memories remain.

Bible examples of mourning for the dead teach us that the days of mourning should be limited. Mourning usually last from seven to thirty days. When Jacob died, Joseph "observed seven days of mourning for his father" Genesis 50:10. "Now when the congregation saw that Aaron was dead all the house of Israel mourned for thirty days" Numbers 20:29. "And the children of Israel wept for Moses thirty days." Deut. 34:8.

Prolonged mourning may indicate the continuation of a soul tie, and the stress of extended grief will create an opportunity for spirits of sorrow, grief and loneliness to enter (this was discussed in chapter six--How Demons Gain Access). Also, if a person attempts to communicate with a deceased loved one, he can easily acquire a demonic spirit.

These soul ties must also be severed in the case of a miscarriage or an abortion.

Demonic Soul Ties Within The Church

Sometimes there are factions within the church that oppose the Body unity. There is an ole hymn that says, "Blessed be the tie that binds our hearts together in Christian love."

There are also evil ties represented by cliques which cause division in the Body. Such groups oppose Church unity and the blending of the Body together.

"But God composed the body, giving greater honor to that part which lacks it, that there should be no schism (division) in the body, but that the members should have the same care for one another." (I Cor. 12:24-25)

Cliques within a church work against the mutual care which Christ designed for His church and, therefore, create ungodly soul ties. The Apostle Paul encountered this same unhealthy soul tie in the church at Corinth. Paul said, "For where there is envy, strife, and divisions among you, are you not carnal and behaving like mere men? For when one says, 'I am of Paul, and another says, 'I am of Apollos, 'are you not carnal? Who then is Paul, and who is Apollos, but ministers whom you believed." I Cor. 3 :3-5).

Paul went on to explain that Christ is the only foundation which can be laid. When man replaces Christ as the foundation, the spirit of Anti-Christ is introduced. This is a spirit we have encountered several times in deliverance. And often the root of that spirit found its beginning in church cliques that brought subsequent division to the church. When the spirit of Anti-Christ is found in the church it is usually indicates division and either a death or near death experience for that church.

Influence of Like Spirits

How do demons enter into soul ties?

Evil spirits are able to enter when spiritual boundaries are violated. God has set which govern our relationships with others. God has given man a nature to love and to live in association with others, but God has set boundaries for all such relationships. For example, there are protective boundaries set by God for marriage. A man is to forsake all others and be joined to his wife. There are similar limitations which govern friendships and bonds within the Body of Christ. When relationships within any area disregard the boundaries which God has established, the relationships become perverse and demons have a legal right to enter. In other words, fleshly soul ties become demonic soul ties.

Through soul ties, a spiritual channel is formed. For example, in a godly marriage, the Holy Spirit flows between husband and wife so that revelations and workings of the Holy Spirit are held in common between a man and his wife. The two become one through the influence of the Holy Spirit (a like spirit). The same principle operates in demonic soul ties. When there is a sinful joining of two individuals, demon spirits in one person open up the other person for similar spirits, and the two are one.

The Power of Soul Ties

The power of soul ties is reflected in two important words in the Greek New Testament: "joined" and "fellowship."

Joined
The word "joined" is used in relation to marriage. In Ephesians 5:31 we are told that a man is to be "joined" with his wife. The literal meaning in Greek is: to cleave, stick to, glue, or cement.

Another use of "joined" is found in Matthew 19:6 where we are told this concerning marriage: Therefore what God has joined together, let no man separate." The word joined can also be translated as "yoked together."

The church is one body. I Corinthians 12:26 says, "And if anyone suffers, all the members suffer with it." That means, whatever happens to one member affects the other members of the Body.

"Do you not know that your bodies are the members of Christ? Shall I then take the members of Christ and make them members of a harlot? Certainly not!" (I Cor. 6:5). Therefore, when a church member engages in sexual immorality, Christ, the head, is affected; and each member of the body is affected. This is the reason that there must be church discipline in such matters to remove any unrepentant sinner. For example, the man in the Corinthian church, who was living incestuously, was to be excommunicated. Paul explained this in I Corinthians 5:6-7:

"Do you not know that a little leaven leavens the whole lump? Therefore, purge out the old leaven, that you may be a new lump."

In addition, the word "joined" also describes our relationship with Christ. "But he who is joined to the Lord is one spirit with Him" (I Cor. 6:17). Just as a husband or wife can commit adultery against his/her spouse, a person can commit adultery against the Lord. Idolatry is spiritual harlotry.

Every occult practice is also an expression of adultery, for by participating in anything occult the person goes outside his relationship with God to receive forbidden knowledge, wisdom, guidance or power. The person who has a relationship with idols is said to have "joined" himself to that idol.

"So Israel was joined to Baal or Peor (an idol of Moab), and the anger of the Lord was aroused against Israel" (Num. 25:3). "They joined themselves also to Baal, and ate sacrifices made to the dead" (Ps. 106:28). "Ephraim is joined to idols, let him alone." (Hos. 4:17).

When a person goes to a fortune teller, he "joins" himself to that occult practitioner by a spiritual connection and, therefore, commits adultery. By spiritual adultery, a spiritual tie is formed. Through occult involvement, one has spiritual intercourse with demons!

Fellowship
We have FELLOWSHIP with Christ through His sacrifice on the cross.

"The cup of blessing which we bless, is it not the communion of the blood of Christ? The which we break, is it not the communion with the body of Christ? For we, being many, are one bread and one body: for we all partake of that one bread" (I Cor. 10:16-17)

The Greek word "fellowship" means: communion, partaking together, sharing in common. We become "one body" by partaking together of the One Bread which is Christ who is broken for us. When we sit at the Lord's Table and partake of the bread and wine of communion, we are partaking of His sacrifice. This is fellowship based on our sharing in His sacrificial death for the atonement of our sins.

We have "fellowship" with demons through idolatry. What happens when we participate in an idolatrous activity such as Ouija board, astrology or divination? We have sat at another table: the table of idols.

"Therefore, my beloved, flee from idolatry... "You cannot drink the cup of the Lord and the cup of demons; you cannot partake of the Lord's Table and the table of demons" (I Cor. 10:14-21).

How does the Lord feel about our fellowship with demons? I Corinthians 10:22 says, *"We provoke the Lord too jealously."* If a wife goes out with another man, the husband is jealous. A Christian's affair with "another spirit" provokes the Lord too jealously. Soul ties likewise, made through occult involvement must be renounced and destroyed.

Husbands and wives who truly become "one flesh" will think alike, act alike and may even look alike. God's Word says that when people are joined to idols they become like their idols.

"Their idols are silver and gold, the work of men's hands. They have mouths, but they do not speak; Eyes they have, but they do not see; They have ears, but do not hear; Noses they have, but they do not smell; They have hands, but they do not handle; feet they have, but they do not walk; Nor do they mutter through their throat. those who make them; so is everyone who trust in them." (Ps. 115:4-8).

Breaking Demonic Soul Ties

Thus far we have seen that demonic soul ties are prevalent and more far-reaching than we have supposed. As evil soul ties are identified, what can be done to reverse their power?

Repentance

Repentance toward God is necessary. God's ordinances have been violated. Lust has taken us beyond the boundaries of purity which the Lord set for us. Even if sin was committed in ignorance, it still requires forgiveness. Just ask God to forgive you for each perverse soul tie which you have created.

Spoil the devil's house by taking back all that he has gained against you.

Confess before God that Satan has no further legal right to you. Declare each demonic soul tie that you have identified is now destroyed in the name of the Lord Jesus Christ.

Command the evil spirits associated with the soul ties to leave you in the Name of Jesus Christ, the Son of God.

Notes

1. Be as specific as possible when breaking soul ties. With regard to soul ties through sexual relationships, remember soul ties are formed with each person with whom you had sex outside of marriage. Name each sexual partner and verbally renounce the ties with each one.

2. Are there soul ties with animals? Are there wrong ties with family members? Are there abnormal ties with pastors or people within the body of Christ? Have spiritual perverse soul ties been created through association with occult activities? If so, ask for forgiveness for each evil soul tie that you have formed. In the name of Jesus, command all demons with perverse soul ties to go.

Chapter Twenty

UNGODLY BELIEF SYSTEMS

Have you ever met someone with an eating disorder such as bulimia or anorexia? No matter how skinny they become, they are convinced that they are fat and need to lose weight. They can hold this view of themselves right up to the moment they die of malnutrition.

Have you ever met a Christian who never felt they were doing enough for God, even though they were one of the most dedicated, active Christians you ever met? Nevertheless, they are convinced that on judgment day they will be found unfaithful and will be cast into hell.

The biggest frustration with these kinds of situations is that no matter how much you tell them the truth or even prove beyond a shadow of a doubt that they are wrong, they still believe the same about themselves. The aforementioned examples are extreme, but it seems their belief is stronger than reality. In fact, that statement is true of all of us.

All of us live by what we believe, no matter whether it is based upon lies or the truth. The truth creates the basis for godly belief systems in our thinking. Consequently, lies are the foundation of ungodly belief systems in our thinking. Either way, the power of what we believe is directly seen in our actions. Lies will blind us to a false reality while Jesus says in John 8:31-32: *"If you abide in My Word, you are My disciples indeed And you shall know the truth and the truth shall make you free."*

In the following pages we are going to discuss what ungodly belief systems are, where they come from and how they can be replaced.

What Are Ungodly Belief Systems?
As human beings, we have been designed to be able to determine what we deem as true and false. We have been given the ability to think, reason and make decisions about our world around us. This ability is closely connected to our capacity to exhibit faith in our decisions.

We are creatures of faith. We all place faith in many things every day. Every time you drive a car, you place faith in the others drivers. Every time you eat in a restaurant, you exercise faith in the cooks not to make you sick. We exercise faith in every aspect of our life and it directly influences our personal and world views.

God made us that way. This is why it is so important for us to base our faith upon truth and not lies. This why Romans 12:2 says; *"And do not be conformed to this world but be transformed by the renewing of your mind, that you may prove what is that good and acceptable and perfect will of God"*

A belief is a conviction, or persuasion that develops over a period of time as we see the world from our own unique perspective. A belief is not necessarily based on facts, but on what we learned and experienced. It is an assumption that certain things are true and real, and that certain things are not true and real. They become like a set of lenses through which we view and interpret life.

Because we are creatures of faith, whether we know God or not, the issue is not whether we operate by belief systems, but on what our belief systems are based.

Unfortunately, many of our belief systems are based on lies. These are ungodly belief systems that lead us to ungodly and often destructive behavior. Even as it says in Proverbs 23:7, *"As a man believes in his heart, so he is,"*. Therefore, what we believe to be true will always (eventually) be evident in what we are on the outside.

Our beliefs create our reality either directly or indirectly.

Therefore, when based upon lies, my beliefs cause me to misinterpret the actions of others, undermine my trust in God, and I become insecure about my circumstances. In the words of Henry Ford, **"If you think you can or you think you can't, you are right."**

Our ungodly beliefs cause us to conclude things that agree with the devil, who is the Father of lies. He wants to rob, kill, and destroy, and lies are his number one tool of accomplishing those goals in our lives. The only defense we have is the truth found in Christ.

Where Do Ungodly Beliefs Come From?
Ever since we were conceived, we have been developing beliefs about ourselves, the people around us, the world around us and God. Since we live in a world marred by sin we often build belief systems upon information that is not in agreement with what God has said. That is why, as Christians, we must constantly allow God and His Word to identify those foundations that are not according to truth upon which we have built our beliefs. Identifying some areas where these lies come in, can help in God showing us which ones are built on lies

The first area is through life's experiences. Whenever we receive a trauma, or are betrayed, or are emotionally wounded, or have any negative experience, it can cause us to assume certain things to be true about that event and all areas of our life related to it.

The earlier in life this happens, the more substantially the assumption will affect the rest of your life. For example, if a person is betrayed by an authority figure young in life it is easier to develop a belief system that all authority figures will betray you. But if it happens after you have had several good authority figures in your life, you are less likely to come to that conclusion.

What this means is that experiences create beliefs, then cause us to expect certain things to happen, which affects our behavior toward others, which may cause them to act in a negative way, which may reinforce our ungodly belief system or even form new ones. This cycle of belief and behavior is always going to be part of our lives.

The second place we can develop ungodly beliefs is from our family. Our family's view about life, politics, religion, education, relationships, etc. molds the way we think about these things before we are able to make our own determinations. Often we are taught to be prejudice, or sarcastic, or aggressive, or timid, or negative. We all tend to believe what we are told by our parents and other relatives. Things like: "You are not as smart, pretty, likeable, etc. as your brother or sister;" "You sure are a poor reader;" or "You sure are clumsy." Such beliefs might be directly and indirectly taught by families, or they may come as a result of the influence of a generational spirit.

The third area is similar to the second, in that we can develop ungodly beliefs from the world around us. Our culture, our peers, the media, modem trends, etc. can all influence us to make determinations about what we believe. The world tells us constantly what is acceptable and not acceptable. It tells us how to get along and fit in. Great pressure is extended on us to meet standards that are set by people who do not know God or His Word. How can we escape?

How Do I Replace Ungodly Belief Systems?

The battle we are talking about here is in the mind. Our enemy knows that if he can convince us of a lie, then he can manipulate our behavior to go against God and His will for us. The scriptures describe the Christian life as a long process of us changing our behavior from the way we used to be without Christ to becoming more and more like His image in our lives. Ephesians 4:20-24 describes the process as taking off the old man (who we were before Christ) and putting on the new man (who we are in Christ). BUT, these are only step 1 and 3 of the process. Step 2 is critical because it is the step that involves us submitting to God and His Word as He renews our minds and our thinking. It is the only step that has a passive verb in it, which means we do not renew our own minds. This puts the emphasis on God to be the One who teaches us. We can identify the old, destructive ways and we can actively practice right behavior, but if we do not let God re-teach us the truth then we will not experience the internal change that God is looking for.

Notice the next verses (Eph. 4:25-32) as examples of what kind of change God is looking for. Look at verse 28 for instance. The command is for thieves to stop stealing, but does that mean they are automatically reformed? When is a thief no longer a thief, to God? When he is no longer stealing?

No, he might just be in between jobs. God says a thief is no longer a thief when (1) He stops stealing; (2) Realizes that there are those with needs (renewing of the mind); and (3) Works to make money to give to the poor.

Do you see then how God wants our outward change to represent a change in thinking, a change in perspective, a change of heart? An alteration in outward behavior is not sufficient and usually doesn't last. When we submit ourselves to the truth as God has revealed it, and allow it to change our understanding about something, then our outward behavior will reflect that understanding as a new belief system. But only the Word of God can make us more and more like Jesus as we follow Him ((John 17:17).

These changes do not occur as we set out on our own to be what the Bible describes as a good Christian. These changes come from the Spirit and through spiritual means to invoke spiritual change in our souls. It is only then that we are transformed instead of just conforming to a set of rules (Romans 12:2). God is not interested in our behavior as much as He is interested in our hearts. He knows that a change of heart will bring about change in behavior. And the battle for that real change is in the mind. That is one reason Paul said in 2 Corinthians 10:5-6:

"For the weapons of our warfare are not carnal, but mighty through God for pulling down strongholds, casting down arguments and every high thing that exalts itself against the knowledge of God, bringing every thought into captivity to the obedience of Christ."

Therefore, our ungodly belief systems must be identified by God through His revealed Word. It is then up to us to allow the truth to replace the lie we have believed.

After this has happened, however; the old way of thinking will often want to return. By the power of the Holy Spirit and in the name of Jesus, we must be diligent to cast down that which power wants to exalt itself against the knowledge of God in our lives. We must give ourselves to the truth as much as we gave ourselves to the lie. In time, the truth will take root and the life of Christ will produce the fruit of righteousness in us. Give yourself to the loving hand of God and trust His truth over your own understanding. It will make you free.

Conclusion

Everything we do is based upon some kind of belief system.

These beliefs about ourselves, the world around us and even God, play a vital role in how we act and respond in life. These beliefs are so powerful that they are often more real than reality itself. If these beliefs are based upon lies, then the behavior they produce in us will often be negative and destructive.

If these beliefs are based upon truth, then they often produce love, peace and joy in our lives. The earlier these beliefs are formed, the more foundational they are to our thinking. But God has given us the power to change even the deepest set of beliefs. We can see real change in our lives, as we let God's Word effect us on the inside. It is our hearts He wants to have full reign in. The body will follow the heart.

The battle, however, is in the mind. As we ask God daily for His truth to be our teacher and we allow Him to show us where we have believed lies, we will find more and more freedom from the bondage of ungodly belief systems.

A Suggested Prayer for Replacing Ungodly Belief Systems

Dear Heavenly Father: I confess my sin of believing that lie that (state the lie, be specific). I thank you that you have shown me that I (state the truth that God has revealed to you) and that this truth I can live by now. I choose to forgive (name those who contributed to the forming of the ungodly belief system) and ask that you would now bless them. I ask You, Lord, to forgive me for receiving this ungodly belief, for living my life based on it, and for anyway I have judged others because of it. I receive Your forgiveness. I also choose to forgive myself for any wasted years while living according to this ungodly belief. Thank You for being the Way, the Truth and the Life.
In Jesus name, Amen.

Chapter Twenty-One

DEMONIC STRONGHOLDS

If you try and cast out demons without removing legal rights and strongholds they are holding onto, then you cannot expect to achieve a completely successful deliverance.

What is a Stronghold?
A stronghold is a faulty thinking pattern based upon lies and deception. Deception is one of the primary weapons of the devil, because it causes one to think in ways that block us from receiving God's best.

Two Very Important Strongholds
1. When you view God incorrectly: One of the most common and devastating strongholds people have is an incorrect image in their mind of who God is, and how He sees us. People, who see God as a taskmaster, live their lives with an unhealthy fear of God.

There is a good kind of fear of God, which is more like a holy respect for Him, and there is another kind of fear that is very unhealthy that the enemy wants us to have. This is the kind of fear where we see God as cruel, cold, distant, and uncaring and will punish us the moment we step out of line.

People who fear they have committed the unpardonable sin are almost guaranteed to have this stronghold. People who find it hard to feel God's love and experience His presence often have this stronghold also. If you feel God is distant and you question if God loves you, then you need to get this stronghold "pulled down."

2. When you view yourself incorrectly: People who suffer from this stronghold have a difficult time seeing the new person that they are now in Christ Jesus, and often suffer from a low self-esteem. They do not fully understand all that Christ has done for them, and how it applies to their life.

Common symptoms of this stronghold are guilty feelings (maybe questioning if they have really been forgiven of their sins), low self-esteem (they feel like sinners, not saints), they lack the spiritual confidence we are supposed to have in Christ Jesus, and overall do not feel worthy spiritually and lack the joy of the Lord in their life.

There are numerous other strongholds (faulty patterns of thinking caused by deception). Things you will discover if you ever get involved in the ministry of deliverance. But the two I have mentioned are very common.

How to tear down a stronghold

"For the weapons of our warfare are not carnal but mighty through God to pulling down strongholds" (2 Cor. 10:4).

Strongholds are always birthed and dwell in deception (lies and ungodly beliefs), so naturally the cure is to bring the truth of God's Word into the picture. You debunk (share the falseness) the lies of the enemy, with the truth, which is the Word of God.

The Bible says that our weapons are mighty for the tearing down of strongholds (2 Cor. 10:4). What is our primary offensive weapon? The sword of the Spirit, which is the Word of God (Eph. 6:17). Truth always dispels deception and lies and therefore the more truth you bring into a situation, the more of the darkness must flee. This is where it is important to continue to grow in God's Word because it is your primary weapon for tearing down the strongholds of deception that the enemy has been feeding you.

In John 8:31-36, Jesus tells us that we can be held in bondage through strongholds in our lives. His solution was to, *"continue in MY Word. ... And you shall know the truth, and the truth shall make you free."* Strongholds are torn down as we meditate on the Word, which is truth.

Chapter Twenty-Two

THE DELIVERANCE MINISTRY AND CHILDREN

Since demon spirits are able to gain entrance into a child, even while in its mother's womb, it is obvious that deliverance should be available to children. God did not put an age limit on deliverance. There are two accounts in scripture of demon possessed children which provide insight into several ideas and principles for the deliverance of children.

* Luke 9:37-42 -- *"Now it happened on the next day, when they came down from the mountain, that a great multitude met Him. Suddenly a man from the multitude cried out, saying, 'Teacher, I implore You, look on my son, for he is my only child. And behold a spirit seizes him, and he suddenly cries out; it convulses him so that he foams at the mouth, and bruising him, it departs from him with great difficulty. So I implored Your disciples to cast it out, but they could not.' Then Jesus answered and said, 'O faithless and perverse generation, how long shall I be with you and bear with you? Bring your son here.' And as he was still coming, the demon threw him down and convulsed him. Then Jesus rebuked the unclean spirit, healed the child, and gave him back to his father."*

* Matthew 15:22-28 -- *"And behold, a woman of Canaan came from that region and cried out to Him, saying, "Have mercy on me, O Lord, Son of David! My daughter is severely demon possessed.' But He answered her not a word. And His disciples came and urged Him, saying; 'send her away, for she cries out after us.' But He answered and said, 'I was not sent except to the lost sheep of the house of Israel.' Then she came and worshiped Him saying, 'Lord, help me!' But He answered and said, It is not good to take the **<u>children's bread</u>** and throw it to the little dogs.' And she said, 'true Lord, but even the little dogs eat the crumbs which fall from their masters' table.' Then Jesus answered and said to her, 'O woman, great is your faith! Let it be to you as you desire.' And her daughter was healed from that very hour."*

These two scriptures show that indeed children can have demons and that faith is the key to deliverance. Neither of these parents had an issue with identifying the source of their child's torment. This differs greatly from most parents' perceptions today. Most parents would act extremely strongly if told that their child was oppressed by an evil spirit. Yet, parents are supposed to be the God-appointed guardian for their children, but unfortunately very few parents correctly take on this responsibility. But now that you have learned how demons enter (Chapter Six), then as parents we can come to know what must be done to protect our children and how to set them free.

Key Truths In Deliverance For Children

Deliverance and corrective punishment are companions.
In addition to casting out demons in children corrective punishment must also be implemented. Proverbs 22:15 says, *"Folly is bound up in the heart of a child, but the rod of discipline will drive it far from him."* Therefore, in addition to casting out a stubborn or rebellious spirit a child must receive consistent discipline. As with adults, unless the flesh is disciplined, the demon and its companions will quickly return.

There are two ways to identify demons in children -- discernment and detection.
Discernment is a gift of the Holy Spirit, and the ability to distinguish between spirits (I Corinthians 12:10). Detection is based upon what you see. If a child is rebellious, it is easy to detect what the problem is, without the immediate need for discernment. This point may seem obvious at first, but remember, younger children cannot properly express themselves verbally, so discernment and detection will be critical.

Parents must take the initiative for their children.
Children cannot directly seek deliverance by or for themselves. It is the parent that must bring them to receive deliverance by Jesus. In the above scripture reading from Luke, the father brought the son, and in the reading from Matthew the mother came to Jesus on behalf of her daughter. The successful deliverance of both children in these scriptures should motivate

parents to receive proper deliverance for their children as soon as possible. While either or both parents can be the ones to bring children for deliverance, having the father present is especially beneficial. God has set the father as head of, and given him authority over, the household. Spirits recognize this also, just as they recognize the authority a husband or wife has over their spouse's demons.

Jesus honors a parents faith.

Both the father and the mother that approached Jesus for deliverance for their children showed faith in Jesus and what He could do for them. In the case of the father, he first went to His disciples and they failed to remove the demon. In the case of the mother, Jesus tested her three times (by silence, by saying He was only sent for the lost sheep of Israel, and by saying that deliverance was only for God's children).

In both situations, the parents faith caused them to continue to pursue deliverance for their children. Jesus greatly values faith, and was indeed upset by the disciples lack of faith in their inability to cast out the demons in the boy. <u>Both those who minister and those coming for deliverance must have faith.</u> Faith is the key to dislodging demons.

A special note on faith. Both seasoned deliverance ministers and parents should not have to have manifestations to build faith. This is especially helpful in dealing with small children. We do not need to be moved by what we see, but by faith and the Word of God, for if faith can move mountains, most assuredly it can cast out demons.

When The Womb Is Unsafe

Satan does not play fair, and how much more unfair can he be than to attack life at its earliest point, when it is least able to defend itself? Satan is called Apollyon, the Destroyer (Revelations 9:11). The devil's options are limited to operating within its legal rights, and must wait for an opening to get into a person's life. Ephesians 4:27 says, *"Do not give the devil a foothold."* How can the devil get a foothold in a child, if still in the mother's womb, and what would open doors of opportunity?

<u>Inherited Curse</u> - Inherited curses give the devil a legal right to be there. As it says in Deuteronomy 5:9, *"I, the Lord your God, am a jealous God punishing the children for the sins of their fathers to the third and forth generations."* (Most bible scholars would agree that the use of numbered generations literally means indefinitely).

Children are born with a few, to many curses based upon the activities of their ancestors. Parents, grandparents, great grandparents, etc have transgressed God's commandments, so the curse has been passed down.

Perhaps there has been idolatry, witchcraft, occult practices, incest, fornication, illegitimacy, adultery or other transgressions in the family tree. Unless these curses have already been disallowed (previously broken), and the demons of these curses expelled, then the devil has the legal right to perpetuate the curse(s) to another generation.

<u>Prenatal Rejection</u> - Another legal right of the devil is when the child is rejected while still in the womb. For example, the baby was not planned, wanted, abortion was considered, complaining about the pregnancy or at any point wishing to not have become pregnant, teenage and illegitimate pregnancies all provide opportunities for demons to enter. In turn they invite spirits of insecurity, rejection, abandonment and other spirits with similar traits.

How do we know this? The devil must abide by the law and means within which God operates, and God and the Holy Spirit most assuredly can operate within the womb. This is clearly stated in Luke 1:15 which says, *"Hadn't an angel of the lord appeared to Zacharias, the father of John the Baptist, and announced that John shall be filled with the Holy Ghost, <u>even in his mother's womb.</u>"*

In the book, "A Manual for Children's Deliverance", there is a story of a woman who initially did not want her child, then decided she did want it, went for deliverance of the child while still in the womb, and the spirit of rejection came out of the baby through the mother in a series of coughs and yawns. After the child was born, the parents reported that he was a quiet and peaceful baby.

It is important to understand that sense a spirit can enter a child at any point starting from conception then deliverance is an option from conception on. The embryonic person can be influenced either in negative or positive ways.

Therefore, if a child in amniotic fluid can be wounded by rejection, he can likewise be nurtured by love and the outward confession of love. Parents should start expressing their love for the child from the moment of conception.

Mother's Addictions - Any addiction the mother may have can also play a major role in the child. Spirits of addiction are transferred from mother to child, although they may lay dormant for years until finding the proper opportunity to attempt to seize control.

Birthing Complications - In Genesis 1:28 we are told to *"Be fruitful and increase in number."* This command of God is something the devil comes against, because he hates fruitfulness and childbearing. With this in mind, when birth takes place, everyone involved should be spiritually vigilant against all possible attacks of the enemy to destroy life, or to hinder or harm mother or child.

DIFFERENCES BETWEEN THE DELIVERANE OF AN ADULT AND A CHILD

Demons in children can be called out in the same way they are called out of an adult, and will usually manifest in the same ways (usually through the mouth and nose). There are, however, some distinct differences:

Communication - Obviously you cannot have an orientation session or counseling session with an infant, newborn or a child under the age of five. This conversation needs to take place with the parent. The deliverance minister must not only use the information provided by the parent, but also must use the gift of discernment of spirits. This coupled with the observance of the child before and during deliverance will also allow for proper detection of influences the enemy has over this child.

The communication technique will change as the child gets a little older. Most children between the ages of 5 or 6 can be given a simple explanation of what you are doing. Specifically they need to know you are not talking to them but a bad spirit in them. Our best experience has been when we explain there are good guys and bad guys in each of us and we are going to tell the bad guys to leave. You could also call them "bad spiritual influences," but never refer to them as demons because the last thing you want to cause is fear.

<u>Cooperation</u> - Most children over the age of five are very cooperative. However, parental authority and discipline measures are sometimes required in younger children in order to gain proper cooperation in the deliverance process. It is a good idea for an infant or younger child to sit with or be held by a parent during deliverance. Although the spirits may cause the child to resist being held.

With older children, it is often easier to address the child, when senses of comfort are taken away. For example, it works well to keep the child and parent separated physically from touching one another. It is also true their siblings should not be present if at all possible.

It should also be noted that demons may cry or scream or show other signs of fear in an attempt to get you the think the child is being hurt or wronged, so that the parent or those ministering deliverance will become sympathetic and stop this deliverance.

Also remember the volume of one's voice does not cause demons to move, it is the name and blood of the Lord Jesus Christ. Therefore, your commands can be calm and matter-of-fact.

Our first deliverance with a child was with a misbehaving (very rebellious) five year old. Initially, the child was agitated and restless and couldn't sit still. But as we prayed and then explained what we were going to do, emphasizing that it would not hurt, she began to calm down some.

We had very little confirmation of the child's deliverance through manifestations but believed by faith the child was delivered. A few days later we received a report that the child's behavior had improved significantly.

Maintaining Deliverance

Parents play a major role in the deliverance of an infant or young child. First, young children know nothing of deliverance. Therefore, parents must observe it and consult with a deliverance team. Second, it is not possible for an infant or a young child to keep themselves free from spirits once they have been delivered. Therefore, this responsibility falls on the parents to be the spiritual guardians of that child.

Children, unlike adults and teenagers, are incapable of protecting themselves from demons, nor engaging in spiritual warfare. Therefore, parent must fill the role of spiritual watchmen and maintain the deliverance for their children.

The casting out of demons is not an instant and complete cure all for all your child's problems. As important and vital as deliverance is, it does not remove parents from their responsibility for their children. Quite the contrary, it underscores the importance of the parent in this area.

As necessary as deliverance may be for most children, it is never a substitute for the needs of that child:

1. Providing a stable home environment:
   ("Train up a child in the way he should go, and when he is old he shall not turn from it.") Proverbs 22:6. Children are deeply affected and personalities
   molded by the emotional and spiritual environment in the home.

2. Providing proper discipline: Deliverance does not take the place of proper discipline, it only supplements it.

3. Providing Love: Both authority and discipline should be dispensed with love. Love is to a family relationship what mortar is to a brick building. Children are God's gift and a sign of His favor.

4. Providing protection, care, affection, tenderness, acceptance and security

Forms of Satanic Oppression/Infestation

Bondage: There are a variety of symptoms in this category and include such things as rebellion, lying, being disrespectful, not forgiving others, frequently displayed anger, being stubborn, deceitfulness, cheating, and the like.

Oppression: Satan will often harass children with a variety of fears. This can cause children to be nervous and anxious for no apparent reason. It is a tactic the enemy uses to oppose any spiritual development in a child.

Afflictions: An evil spirit can cause children to have accidents, difficulties, frequent illnesses and allergies of all kinds.

Parents Often Bring Oppression To Their Children: Many parents overlook the fact that they may be the basic cause of their children's problems. Frequently parents must first free themselves of their own problems before assisting with the deliverance of their child. Deliverance with children often begins when the parents themselves start seeking deliverance from demonic influence. Therefore, we prefer, and always recommend, that a parent goes through deliverance before having their child experience deliverance.

Who Should Participate in a Childs Deliverance?
As with any deliverance, doubters SHOULD NEVER be present during anyone's deliverance, since they can not only hinder the deliverance process but open themselves up to transfer spirits (evil spirits being ejected may transfer themselves to an unsuspecting doubter or unbeliever).

It is always wise to have those experienced in deliverance present. However, parents who have themselves already been delivered and have received training should take the lead as they have more authority to pray for their own children than anyone else because they are the child's spiritual covering. Otherwise always have a trained minister take the lead.

How to Pray For a Child
If the child is of sufficient age and maturity to understand what he is doing, guide them in renouncing his/her sins in prayer. If, however, the child is not

cooperative the parent should renounce for them.

The process for deliverance should be the same as with adults.
Always take a history and list the problems the child deals with: rejection, rebellion, anger, addictions, mental problems, and so forth. But in addition be led by the Holy Spirit and the gift of discernment. Then just command those spirits, in Jesus name, to leave that child one by one. For example, "spirit of rebellion, I command you in the name of Jesus to leave this child."

As you progress through a deliverance session be sure to name each spirit and command them to leave in Jesus' name.

Final Action

Thank the Lord for His faithfulness, His work on the cross and for coming to destroy the works of the devil. Then lay hands on the child and ask the Lord to cleanse each part of that child's personality where a demon has lived (mind, heart, will and different parts of the body).

Then ask the Lord to fill the child with His love, His presence, and His peace. Finally, ask for complete healing, emphasizing any part of the body that was affected.

Consistent prayer over the child is essential. They are not only vulnerable to the enemy but they are also more receptive and tend to absorb positive spiritual influences easier than adults. So through consistent prayer and guidance parents should continually expose their children to God's Word and the touch of His presence.

Chapter Twenty-Three

NECESSARY STEPS TO DELIVERANCE

Prior to anyone requesting deliverance an individual should take a personal inventory and be prepared to meet the necessary conditions outlined in this chapter. Submitting to a deliverance ministry prior to acknowledging and submitting to these steps will greatly hinder both the process and results of deliverance. In fact, any reputable deliverance minister should require these steps of anyone they take through deliverance.

Honesty

An individual must be honest with himself and with God if he expects to receive God's blessing of deliverance. If one is dishonest it will keep areas of one's life in darkness.

Demon spirits thrive on darkness but honesty helps bring them into the light. Any non-confessed or un-repented sin gives a demon a "legal right" to remain. Prior to starting the interview process asks God to help you see yourself as He sees you and to bring to light anything that is not of Him.

"I acknowledge my sin to You, and my iniquity I have not hidden. I said, I will confess my transgressions to the Lord, and You forgave the iniquity \ of my sin." Psalm 32:5

"Search me, Oh Lord, and know my heart; try me (test me), and know my anxieties; and see if there is any wicked way in me. And lead me in the way of everlasting." Psalm 139:23-24

Humility

With regard to deliverance humility involves recognition that one is dependent upon God and His provisions for deliverance.

"God resists the proud, but gives grace to the humble. Therefore, submit to God. Resist the devil and he will flee from you." James 4:6b-7

Humility also requires a complete openness with God's servants ministering deliverance.

"Confess your trespasses one to another, and pray for one another, that you may be healed." James 5:16a

Repentance
Repentance is a decision to turn from your sins and from Satan. It requires a complete changing of your mind about sin so that you hate evil and want no part of it in your life.

The purpose of deliverance is not to merely gain relief from your problems but to become more like Jesus through obedience to all that God requires. Repentance is a turning from all that hinders spiritual growth, ministry and fellowship. Repentance requires open confession of all sin. It takes away the legal rights of demon spirits.

Forgiveness
Scripture is clear that God forgives everyone who confesses their sins and ask for forgiveness.

"If we confess our sins, He is faithful and just to forgives us our sins and cleanses us from all unrighteousness." (I John 1.-9)

God also expects us to forgive everyone who has ever wronged us in any way.

"For if you forgive men their trespasses your heavenly Father will also forgive you. But if you do not forgive men their trespasses, neither will your Father forgive you your trespasses." Matt. 6:14-15

The willingness to forgive is absolutely essential for one to receive deliverance. No deliverance minister can effectively bring deliverance unless the candidate has met God's conditions, and this includes forgiving others.

Prayer
Prior to beginning the actual deliverance the candidate must ask God to deliver them and set them free in the name of Jesus. Most deliverance ministers will lead you in such a prayer.

".. whoever calls on the name of the Lord shall be delivered."
Joel 2:3

Warfare
Prayer and warfare are two separate and distinct activities. Prayer is toward God and warfare is toward the enemy. Our warfare against demon powers is not fleshly but spiritual (Ephesians 6:10-12 and 2 Corinthians 10:3-5). Use the weapons of submission to God, the blood of Jesus Christ, the Word of God, and your testimony as a believer (James 4:7; Rev. 12:11; Eph. 6:17).

Identify the spirits, address them directly by name in a commanding voice, and in faith command them to go in the name of Jesus. Enter the battle with determination, confidence and assurance of victory. Christ will not fail! He is the deliver!

"And these signs will follow those that believe; In My name they will cast out demons..." Mark 16:17a

"Behold I give you the authority to trample on serpents and scorpions, and over all the power of the enemy, and nothing by any means shall hurt you." Luke 10.19

"The Lord is my rock and my fortress and my deliverer."
Psalm 18:2

Chapter Twenty-Four

THE DELIVERANCE TEAM

Jesus established the pattern of team work for His disciples. When He sent out His twelve disciples to minister He sent them out in twos. When He commissioned the seventy He also sent them out by twos.

Other ministry teams are found in the Book of Acts. On the first missionary journey there were Paul, Barnabas and John Mark. Later there was Paul and Silas. Aquilla and Priscilla were a husband and wife team. Team ministry is a principle in Scripture and it is especially suitable and effective in the deliverance ministry.

Size and Composition

There is no ideal number for a deliverance team, and every situation is different. The rule of thumb is that no less than two and no more than six. Both men and women should be present.

Because of the unusual facets of this ministry, a man should never minister alone to a women or a women to man. Also, the laying on of hands is often required during deliverance and therefore both men and women should be present, as men and women should not lay hands on the opposite sex indiscriminately. Another reason for having both sexes present is that there are times, although it is not typical, when someone must be physically restrained.

Although we do not war against flesh and blood, the demons may demonstrate themselves violently at times, so that the person experiencing deliverance must be restrained from injuring himself or others.
One individual will always take the lead in deliverance while others pray quietly in the Spirit. If someone other than the individual calling out demons gets a "word from God" or "discerns a specific spirit" is present, they should write it down and give it to the person leading the deliverance.

There will always be times when other members of the team need to take a lead role but only after discussing this with the team leader.

Team Unity

Unity on the deliverance team is absolutely essential. Satan will capitalize on any disunity. In fact, he will attempt to bring disunity to the deliverance team using a variety of methods. A demon may even speak to the team something like, "only one of you is really following the Lord, the rest of you are tag-a-longs" or "one of you doesn't really believe in deliverance." The enemy will use anything to try and bring doubt about one another and thereby bring disunity.

Any group that works together must learn to flow with the Spirit and have confidence in one another. When you are in the midst of battle with demon spirits it is not the time to have a disagreement. For example, someone may think they discern a specific demon and others may disagree. This is not the time for a discussion on the accuracy or to challenge someone's spiritual discernment. It is best to just challenge the spirit discerned and if it is there "you'll get it." Always remember that an occasional mistake will probably be made in discernment, but this will not have a negative effect on the overall deliverance. Teams are built on trust.

Functions of Team Members

With the exception of needing a "team leader" assigned to the calling out of demons during the deliverance process there are no specific rules. The team leader is required to maintain order but in lengthy deliverance sessions it is not unusual for the lead person to change. That person should, however, be designated in advance.

It is imperative that each member of the team be sensitive and obedient to the leading of the Holy Spirit. Team members not calling out demons should be in quite prayer, reading scripture or manning the bucket should one be needed.
Remember, the purpose is to set the captive free and give glory to Jesus, so it makes no difference who is leading the warfare. Each person present is equally important.

Chapter Twenty-Five

OBSTACLES TO DELIVERANCE

The following teaching is presented with the prayer and hope that anyone with unsettled questions that have prevented them from involvement in deliverance will gain understanding and be able to go forth in obedience to the Lord. God has not called us to debate deliverance but to do it! For, "these signs will follow them that believe; In My name they will cast out demons."

There are numerous myths, misunderstandings, and misinformation concerning the ministry of deliverance. The first battle ground is the mind, where Satan has sown questions, doubts and fears which become hindrances to involvement in this valid, biblical ministry established by Jesus Himself.

Do not spend your time with individuals who are un-teachable and argumentative. Jesus sometimes gave a simple, straightforward answer to His critics, then spent His time ministering to those who were receptive and to teaching His disciples. We would be wise to follow His example.

We can spend time with those who truly desire answers because ignorance, prejudice and fear are hurdles that some sincere Christians must overcome before they are willing to become involved in spiritual warfare. We have a responsibility to teach them. However, do not waste time on those who are un-teachable and argumentative.

The only way to deal with the devil and his demons is through direct confrontation. Know also, that God has given the Christian and His church the commission to cast out demons (Matt. 10:1; Luke 10:17-19; Mark 16:17). Some believers have false opinions that prevent them from accepting deliverance as a vital ministry. Before anyone can bring himself to obedience to deal with the devil and demons, the obstacles in this chapter must be overcome in an individual's mind.

OBSTACLES AND UNTRUTHS

<u>Fear At The Mention of Demons, The Devil And Deliverance.</u>
1. The concept of demons held by many has been from fiction, mythology and superstition rather than from scripture. The fear that some have of deliverance has come from in part through movies like "The Exorcist" and "Rosemary's Baby" which were designed to create mystery, sensationalism, violence and fear rather than to the truth.

2. The Christian should look at the resources available to them and know that their power and authority in the name of Jesus is far greater than that of the enemy. Light dispels darkness. Fear and terror will leave when people embrace the truth. Faith overcomes fear. Romans 10:17ef:

<u>Unbelief: There Is No Such Thing As The Devil and Demons</u>
Incorrect concepts of the devil have been programmed by the world, which is controlled by Satan himself. He is not running around in a red suit with a long pointed tail carrying a pitchfork. He is not the ruler over hell, but one day he will become the chief resident in hell.   (Rev.20:10)

The Bible is filled with the truth about Satan and his demon spirits. Jesus said, *"You shall know the truth and the truth shall make you free* (John 8:32)

If we expect to be free we must know the truth about the devil. The Bible must be the basis for our beliefs.

<u>Demons Are Real, But Too Powerful For Us To Confront</u>
1. There is no doubt that the devil has power and weapons he uses against Christians, but he does not have unlimited access to our lives.

2. Jesus defeated Satan through the cross and resurrection. We are seated with Christ and have power over the devil.   (Ephesians 1:18-27)

3. As believers in Jesus Christ we have complete authority and power over the devil and demons (Luke 9:1; 10:19)

Deliverance is Valid; However, It Should Be Left To Experts

1. Who is an expert? It is true that a Christian should have knowledge and understanding about demons and deliverance. It is also true that everyone involved in this ministry should attempt to become an expert. But what does the Bible tell us?

2. Christ's commission is given to the whole church. Mark 16:17 says that those who believe shall cast out demons.

Deliverance is part of the Gospel of salvation which is for the whole man — spirit, soul and body. Casting out demons is a simple, basic sign that should accompany the ministry of every witnessing spirit-filled believer. (Mark 16:15,17)

Christians Cannot Have Demons

In the Bible there is no distinction made between believers and unbelievers having demons. The reason: both can have demons.

Deliverance is called the "Children's Bread" (Matt. 15:21-28; Mark 7:24-30), which means it is for God's own Sons and daughters; purchased by the blood of Jesus. Therefore, a distinction IS MADE as to who is qualified for deliverance. It is for God's children.

When demons are cast out of a person, the "house" must be filled. (Matt.12:43-45). How could an unbeliever fill his house? He is void of spiritual resources.

The Christian is the Temple of the Holy Spirit:

There are three areas of the Temple, and there are three areas in us: Body, Soul and Spirit. The body, soul and spirit are parallel to the Outer Court, The Holy Place and the Holy of Holies. When the Temple was dedicated, God's presence indwelled the Holy of Holies. When we are saved, our spirits are quickened and indwelled by God.

In other words the Holy Spirit lives in our spirit and not in our body or soul, which is where demon reside.

Jesus cleansed the temple. He "cast out" all that deified the Temple, but only the outer court needed cleansing. It had become a "den of thieves." God's presence was in the Temple in the Holy of Holies.

Deliverance and healing are provisions of God's atoning blood. Mark 8:16-17. If it were impossible for Christians to have a demon, then neither could we become sick, because both healing and deliverance are benefits of the cross. Mark 8:16-17

It is better to acknowledge that you have a demon (if you do), and cast it out rather than deny you have a demon and keep it.

II Corinthians 10:3-5 is addressed to Christians who have strongholds in their minds. The remedy requires spiritual weapons to pull down the devils strongholds.

II Corinthians 11:4 is a warning to Christians that it is possible to "receive another spirit" other than the Holy Spirit.

Demons Have No Activity In Civilized Countries. They Are Active Only In Remote Countries Where Witchcraft and Idolatry Prevail.

1. Demonic activity is intense in countries where witchcraft and idolatry prevail. However, witchcraft and the occult have made great inroads into civilized countries.

2. There are many activities of demons other than through witchcraft and the occult.

3. This is one of Satan's deceptions. As long as someone thinks he is too intelligent or cultured to be demonized, he is blind to how demons gain entrance and how they function.

They Will Come Back Seven Times Worse
The Bible does not teach that they WILL come back in greater numbers and force, but that it is POSSIBLE for them to do so.

It is true that we need to be wise as to whom we minister deliverance. A lost person has no way to "fill his house" and therefore, is not candidate for deliverance. Nor should we minister deliverance to a doubting Christian as it is unlikely they could stand in their deliverance.

Deliverance Must Never Be Done In Public
Jesus consistently cast out evil spirits in public. There is no clear biblical reference to private deliverance. However, due to the nature, process and length of most deliverances many individuals prefer that it be done in private.

Many reject public deliverance because of fear: Fear how demons may manifest; fear how others might view them; fear that others might be offended; fear of things getting out of control, and fear of embarrassment These fears can cause a hindrance and even failure of that individual's freedom. Also, anyone who doubts deliverance should not be present because: (a) They give the enemy strength, and (b) they open themselves up to transfer spirits.

Deliverance Is Just A Matter Of Faith
This statement usually indicates that this person believes that if you have enough faith then God will automatically take care of all demons. BUT, God has given us authority and responsibility to deal with demons directly; His work is done.

Faith IS important to deliverance, for we must believe that when we speak to a demon it must obey. Demons know when we do not have faith and take advantage of it. (Acts19:13-17)

The disciples were unable to cast out a certain demon because of their unbelief. Fasting and prayer builds faith to cast out demons. (Mark 17:14-21)
"Faith, without works is dead" James 2:17. The person who has an active faith will speak to the "mountain."

Demonization should be considered a mountain to be

removed by speaking in faith.   (Mark 11:22-23)

Passive faith is contrary to the scriptural command that we are to engage in warfare and "wrestle" against principalities and powers, "resist" the devil and "cast out" demons.

Deliverance Glorifies The Devil. We Should Keep Our Minds on Jesus

This may sound good, but it is false reasoning. The Bible DOES NOT teach us to ignore the devil but to confront, resist, wrestle, stand against and cast him out.

Jesus is glorified when we engage in spiritual warfare because we are exalting His name, His precious blood, and His Word. Satan gets no glory through being defeated. All the glory goes to the One who is stronger than the devil.

Jesus Did It All For Us. We Don't Have To Fight

The devil would like us to adopt this position. It means he can continually work against us without challenge.

There is a widespread misunderstanding as to what is meant by Jesus defeating the devil. Jesus did not destroy the devil; he destroyed the "works" of the devil (1 John 3:8).

The devil has not yet been chained and put into the bottomless pit. He is still "roaming around" (1 Peter 5:8). He remains the "god of this world" (II Cor. 4:4), where he rules as *"the prince of the power of the air"* (Eph. 2:2).

Chapter Twenty-Six

DELIVERANCE FROM SELF

This chapter is not about self-deliverance but deliverance from self. That is, removing the demonic spirits associated with self-indulgence or selfishness, and dying to self in all life' circumstances.

It is only through the death of self that someone can experience complete deliverance.

During the past twenty-seven years of deliverance ministry we have seen people set free from nearly every imaginable sort of bondage: addictions, lust, perversions, unforgiveness, rebellion, hurts, double-mindedness, fears, rejection, curses, doubt & unbelief, anger, rage, religious spirits, and on and on. However, we are convinced that the greatest need is for deliverance of "self."

It seems that most people are all wrapped up and absorbed by their own problems, circumstances, ambitions and feelings. Their entire being is only concerned with "self."

Because of this they disregard the first and greatest commandment: "Love the Lord your God with all your heart and with all your soul and with all your mind. This is the first and greatest commandment" (Matt. 22:37).

The devil has a master plan to capture all mankind. It appears to us that this plan is the same for every person—imprisonment in self. Self is the devil's chief ally and man's number one enemy.

I am not taking away from the damage and torment done by demonic spirits nor the need for them to be cast out. But we must remove self also because self keeps the believer from becoming a true disciple of Christ. Jesus Himself declared; *"...whoever of you does not forsake all that he has* **cannot** *be My disciple."* (Luke 14:33).

Self, whether it is self-pity, self-indulgence, self-pleasure, self-anything, will hinder our living up to our potential. If we become all that we can be in Christ, we become a powerful influence for God's kingdom. This is what the devil fears, so he does all he can to prevent us from reaching maturity and fulfilling our calling in Christ. The devil's objective is to get the believer so occupied with self that we lose our spiritual saltiness: That is, our ability to influence whomever we contact.

"Salt is good; but if the salt has lost its flavor (saltiness) how shall it be seasoned? It is neither fit for the land nor for the dunghill, but men throw it out" (Luke 14:33-34).

Selfishness takes the saltiness (flavor) out of Christians. Selfishness not only impedes our maturing in Christ but it also destroys marriages, families, and churches. Are we not commanded to esteem others higher than ourselves?

Consider the believer's great potential. When one receives Christ as Lord and Savior they become equipped with the power of spiritual discernment. Specifically, according to John 3:3 they can "see (discern) the kingdom of God." The unbeliever does not accept the things that come from the Spirit of God because they are foolishness to him, and he cannot understand them, because they are spiritually discerned. (I Cor. 2:14)

In addition to our power to discern the spiritual realm, Jesus promised that *"You will have power when the Holy Spirit comes upon you."* (Acts 1:8).

Therefore, spirit-filled believers (those with the subsequent experience of the baptism in the Holy Spirit—the promise of the Father) have the potential to function in supernatural power. We are given power to heal the sick, cast out demons, speak in new tongues, interpret tongues, prophesy, and perform miracles.

After Pentecost, the disciples ministered in the power of the Holy Spirit as it says in Acts 5:12, *"And through the hands of the apostles many signs and wonders were done among the people."*

This is the potential of every spirit-filled believer. However, some were defeated by selfishness. Ananias and Sapphira coveted and lied, and their lives and ministry ended. Simon, a converted sorcerer, wanted the power of the Holy Spirit for personal gain and Peter rebuked him saying, *"You have neither part nor portion in this matter, for your heart is not right in the sight of God."* (Acts 8:21)

Every believer is a member of Christ's spiritual body, the church, and is REQUIRED to die to self in order to fulfill God's purpose for them in the body of Christ. However, the body (church) cannot function properly when its members fall into Satan's trap of "self". Self causes us to either think of ourselves as inadequate or superior in comparison with others. (see I Cor. 12:14-27).

You may be thinking, is he saying that every demonic problem entails a problem with self? The answer is yes. For example: The person wounded with rejection becomes conscious of "self" because of self hurts. Until one becomes secure in God's love, and can love others, even his enemies, he will remain in bondage to self. Lust is self-gratification and self-indulgence; rebellion is self rule; fear is self-concern; resentment is self-vindication, witchcraft is self- advantage, pride is self-exaltation. Every demon that can be named has a synonym name with a "self" prefix.

Therefore, deliverance does not come solely from casting out demons; the "self thing" that gives place to these demons must also be removed. This is accomplished by dying to self. For this reason after deliverance we talk with the individual on how to stand in their deliverance---not giving place to the devil nor the flesh.

Many Bible heroes initially had self-problems, and only after their self-problems were remedied were these men useful to God. Moses was bound by inferiority. He felt unqualified for the task that God had for him. Gideon also felt inadequate. He considered himself the least person in all Israel. David yielded to self-indulgence and committed adultery. Saul was a self-righteous Pharisee and a persecutor of Christians. But each of these men were delivered from self and greatly used of God.

Revelation 12:11 says, *"They overcame him (Satan) by the blood of the Lamb, and the word of their testimony; and they did not love their own lives to the death."*

In the above verse, three spiritual weapons are named which every believer has available to defeat the devil. Most Christians only refer to the first two, but we need to take a close look at all three.

First, believers in Jesus can utilize the power inherent in His incorruptible blood. The blood becomes a weapon when we testify what the blood of Jesus has done for us through its justifying, sanctifying, redeeming and atoning power. The devil is put to flight when we remind him that we have taken refuge in the shed blood of Jesus.

The second weapon named is "the word of our testimony", which means the testimony of Jesus Christ. (Rev. 12:17) We actually utilize the weapon of testimony when we declare who Jesus is: That He is the sinless Son of God who left His throne in glory, became incarnate, was tempted in all ways and yet was without sin. That He went to the cross and laid down His life for us as sinners, rose from the dead, ascended to His throne at the right hand of the Father and is coming again in His glory and power.

The believer's third weapon, which is death to self, seems a bit strange. The last part of Rev. 12:11 says; *"they did not love their lives to the death."* When understood, this is an especially powerful weapon, yet for the most part it is neglected. Jesus overcame the devil. The victory of the cross was assured in Gethsemane, when He prayed, "Father...not as I will, but as You will." He is our example. He demonstrated that we can defeat the enemy with the same weapon. The devil has no advantage over a person who has died to self. Again, Jesus as our example, died to self when He said; Your will, not My will be done.

To help understand this concept, suppose a person is delivered from all demonic spirits. What is left? Only his real self is left. What then must that person do with the real self? It must be crucified: taken to the cross and put to death! Because only as self dies can Christ come forth in us. Only through death to self can one experience the full extent of deliverance. Again, this chapter is not to diminish any aspect of deliverance or the need to cast out demons. But every believer must realize that self is also an equally important aspect of becoming and remaining free from the clutches of Satan.

Satan knows that his destructive plans for a person are nullified when a person dies to self in order to serve Christ. Therefore, the devil's strategy is to entice us to set our own agenda and follow selfish pursuits instead of being committed to God's purposes.

This strategy is very clear in scripture where we find two classic examples of temptation: the temptations of Eve and of Jesus.
How did the serpent temp Eve? He tempted her to set aside God's command and gratify self. What three avenues of temptation did he employ? The same as those stated in I John2:16 — the lust of the flesh, the lust of the eyes, and the pride of life.

"The woman saw that the fruit of the tree was for food" — this appealed to the lust of her flesh *"And was pleasing to the eyes"*-this appealed to the lust of the eyes. *"And desirable for gaining Wisdom"*— this touched her pride. (See Genesis 3:6).

The devil's three-pronged temptations of Jesus followed exactly the same pattern. (Matthew Il). He tempted Christ to turn stones into bread in order to gratify the lust of the flesh. He further tempted Jesus through the lust of the eyes by showing Him the kingdoms of the world and their glory and offering them to Him in exchange for His worship.

The third temptation appealed to the pride of life: Jesus was urged to leap from the pinnacle of the temple, depending upon angels to catch Him, thus making a public display that would draw men's attention and admiration.

Ever since Eden, Satan has continued to use the same three temptations to draw men and women out of their devotion to God and into self-idolatry.

If Jesus had yielded to any one of those temptations it would have disqualified Him from becoming our Savior. He would have sinned. Why? Because He would have abandoned the Father's will in preference to fulfilling His own desires. This is the problem many Christians have today; we abandon God's will for us to satisfy our own desires. Jesus is our example and He never acted independently of the Heavenly Father.

The three Persons of the Godhead never act independently of one another. Likewise, in order for us to have total victory over the devil and his demons, we cannot act independently of God This is why the Bible tells us in James 4:7; *"Submit to God. Resist the devil and he will flee from you."*

How do we submit to God? We accomplish this through the submission of our own will. Only through this kind of surrender can we completely and effectively resist the devil.

The goals of deliverance include identifying and breaking curses, riding oneself of unforgiveness, breaking sole ties, renouncing any participation in the occult, renouncing ungodly beliefs and casting out evil spirits. But the ultimate goal of deliverance goes beyond these things

We must identify the devil's schemes and shut the door against him. We must remain determined to keep demons out and not allow them to return. This is best achieved when one has victory over self.

The process is much easier after deliverance, but non-crucified self gives demons an opportunity to take up residence in our lives.

The Apostle Paul expressed his formula for victory in these words: *"I have been crucified with Christ, it is no longer I who live, but Christ lives in me; and the life that I now live in the flesh I live by faith in the Son of God, who loved me and gave Himself for me."* (Gal. 2:20)

The key is this: Every demon either pulls down or puffs up "self". When self gets the attention God is no longer central in your life. That is why deliverance is not complete until we willingly deny our flesh (self).

"Anyone who does not take his cross and follow Me is not worthy of Me. He who finds his life will lose it, and he who loses his life for My sake will find it." (Matt. 10:38-39)

Chapter Twenty-Seven

SPIRITUAL HOUSECLEANING

Admittedly, deliverance practices are taken to extremes sometimes. I have heard of people dressing in sweatshirts and sweat pants because they planned to physically wrestle with demons. They obviously don't know their authority as a believer. Other people are convinced there are demons lurking under every rock and behind every bush just waiting to pounce on them.

The purpose of this chapter is not to take deliverance to an extreme. But, throughout our years in this ministry, we have seen believers who are under persistent attack without understanding why. We have found that it is often because they have given the enemy legal rights to their home by keeping objects and other things that originate in the occult.

"Therefore, the children of Israel could not stand before their enemies, but turned their backs before their enemies, because they have become doomed to destruction. Neither will I be with you anymore, unless you destroy the accursed from among you. Get up, "sanctify the people, and say, thus says the Lord God of Israel: There is an accursed thing in your midst, O Israel; you cannot stand before your enemies until you take away the accursed thing from among you." (Joshua 7:12-13)

"Thus it became known both to all the Jews and Greeks dwelling in Ephesus; and fear 'fell upon them all, and the name of the Lord was magnified. And many who had believed came confessing and telling their deeds" (Acts 19:17-18)

The point to this is that places, like a house or a church, can be contaminated. For our purposes we are going to consider someone's home.

Symptoms of a House that is Spiritually Contaminated
These symptoms include frequent illness, nightmares, constant fighting and divisions, lack of peace, demonic appearances, and movement of objects with no explanation, bad orders, habitual nausea, and headaches.

"For once you were darkness, but are now light in the Lord. Walk as children of light. (for the fruit of the Spirit is in all goodness, righteousness, and truth), proving what is acceptable to the Lord. And have no fellowship with the unfruitful works of darkness, but rather expose them." (Ephesians 5:8-11).

Sometimes we wonder why certain things happen (or continue to happen) in our homes. Often, the reason is because objects of demonic origin are being kept there.

During our travels we have found this to be true on several occasions. One of the most interesting was a women who had been experiencing sexual attacks at night by an unseen entity. We were called to the home through a mutual acquaintance. After praying in each room of the house, and not sensing anything, we ended up in a family room where most of these attacks occurred.

There on the wall was a collection of American Indian Witchdoctor Dolls which caused the hair on our bodies to stand on end. It was obvious that this was the source of the problem.

Items That Need to be Removed and Destroyed
* Materials used in witchcraft or occult activities
* Antiques with unknown backgrounds
* Materials and games such as Ouija boards, dragon games, Buddha figures, yoga books and Hindu objects.
* Artifacts of oriental worship, New Age books
* Quartz stones, items used for good luck
* The rosary, figures of saints
* Astrology books, Tarot cards, crystal ball and pendulums
* CDs, cassettes and posters of rock music
* Arts, crafts and pictures with demonic representations
* Material related to sects such as Mormons, Jehovah's Witnesses, and Freemasonry
* Souvenirs from other countries that contain images of

idols
* Demonic, violent, pornographic movies and video
* Good luck charms, fetishes or religious objects
* Images or statutes of angels, or elephants used for good luck
* Images that represent the goddess Diana, queen of heaven
* Any item used in idolatry will almost certainly have a spirit attached to it. If that object is brought into your home that demonic spirit can operate against the people

It is very important to clean our homes. Some objects are obviously occultic and defiled, get rid of them. Some objects are completely not, don't worry about them. Some objects, you may not be sure about. These are the ones you ask the Lord what to do with. However, I usually suggest that you go through your house, looking through all the closets and rooms, asking the Holy Spirit to show you what things are not pleasing to God. Then throw them away or burn them.

At this point it is best to walk through your home room by room and command any unclean spirits to leave your home and property

Chapter Twenty-Eight

DEMON GROUPINGS

Demons are identified by their nature. A demon of anger is called "anger." Each demon is a specialist. An anger demon cannot cause lust, he can only promote anger. Therefore, the function, or nature, of a demon is also how it is identified (its name). For example, a spirit that causes rebellion goes by the name of rebellion; a spirit that causes rejection is called rejection, and so on.

There are exceptions to this when a demon takes on a personal name or a foreign name to deceive the deliverance minister and keep him from "finding" it. Therefore, at times it may be necessary to ask the demon its name, nature or function.

Indwelling spirits are seldom found alone; they group together in colonies or families. During both the interview and deliverance process you will identify or discern specific demons. As this happens you should be on the lookout for its companions. These groupings will become more and more familiar as you get more and more involved in the deliverance ministry. However, it is also a good idea to become familiar with demon groupings in advance.

There is no right or wrong grouping and each deliverance minister usually has his own groupings. However, you will notice that all groupings follow a very logical pattern.

Certain types of spirits are found over and over in the same combination; however, these combination are not always the same.

<u>The possibilities for groupings are almost unlimited</u>
Within each grouping there will be a "strong man" or ruling spirit. Often during deliverance that strongman will be specifically identified. But, contrary to what some have suggested, it is not always necessary to identify

the ruling spirit in order to have an effective deliverance.

Typically we find that the ruling spirit (strongman) is usually the first spirit to invade a certain demon grouping. Because he is the first to enter he establishes himself as the ruler. He then becomes the key to opening the way for other spirits to enter. Therefore, we often bind (spiritually) several demons in a grouping together and cast them out together thereby, getting the strong man and his companions. There are also times when the ruler must be separated from his companions as they draw strength from the strongman and can be more difficult to cast out.

Although demons typically follow a pattern, demon groupings are not absolute. For example, you may find a spirit of anger in the bitterness family. It is also possible to find a specific demon in more than one category or family grouping. For example, depression may be found in an infirm spiritual grouping and in a grouping under rejection.

Some individuals believe that there are only three strongmen: **Bitterness, Greed, and Sexual Immorality** and all indwelling demons fit within one of these categories.

Others suggest that there are twelve separate demon groupings we could consider as strongmen or rulers. These would include spirits **of Infirmity, Fear, Divination, Whoredom, Bondage, Haughtiness, Perverseness, Anti-Christ, Heaviness, Lying, Jealously, and Error.**

Frank and Ida Hammond, authors of the book Pigs in the Parlor, suggest 52 different groupings. Personally, we place them in about 37 different groupings. Groupings are helpful when identifying specific demons and they assist you in the deliverance process as it helps keep you within the appropriate grouping until that area is cleansed.

We often give those who desire deliverance a list of demon groupings to help them identify the strongmen in their life and the corresponding evil spirits. A sample of this document is listed at the end of this chapter.

The key to identifying spirits and specific groupings is taking a complete history (discussed later), and not just rely on the grouping survey completed by the person receiving deliverance. It is also important to listen to the Holy Spirit and follow His lead during the deliverance process. If you are in tune with the Spirit of God He will direct you as to what demons should be addressed and in what order. He will also, at times, direct you to bind certain demons in a group together so you can cast them out as a group.

The demon groupings listed in this chapter are simply suggestions as to what you may encounter.

These are not an exhaustive listing nor are these groupings cast in stone, and several evil spirits can, and will, be found under various strongmen headings. What is presented in the following pages is what we have discovered during our deliverance ministry. Others in this ministry may group them differently based upon their experiences in that house.

Common Indications That a House Needs Cleansing
There are others but these are the most common:
* Unexplained sounds or voices at night
* Someone walking
* Doors opening or closing
* Rattling chains
*Objects moving without anyone touching them
* Spirit beings appearing at night
* Unexplained areas of coldness in the house

DELIVERANCE GROUPINGS

Please Circle Those Items Which
Are Strongholds in Your Life

Rejection
Hurt
Deep Hurt
Wounded Spirit
Abandonment
Fear of Rejection
Self-rejection
Desertion
Rejection
Insecurity
Inferiority
Uselessness

Control
Jezebel
Witchcraft
Dominance
Possessiveness
Manipulation
Pride (I know best
Selfishness

Anxiety
Burden
Fatigue
Heaviness
Nervousness
Restlessness
Weariness
Worry
Tension

Fears
Mental Torment
Over Sensitivity
Fear of (name)
   illness)
Fear of man
Fear of Demons
Sudden Fear
Hidden Fear
Fear of Dark
Fear of Authority
Sudden Fear

Bitterness
Resentment
Hatred
Unforgiveness
Violence
Temper
Retaliation
Murder
Complainer
Gossip

Jealously
Envy
Suspicion
Distrust

Deception
Confusion
Lying

Emotional Bondage
Instability
Have no Purpose
No Direction
No Goals
Procrastination
Time Waster
Indecision
Lack of
   Confidence

Rebellion
Self-will
Stubbornness
Disobedience
Independence
Disrespectful
Bull-headed

Abandonment
Isolation
Loneliness
Feeling Unwanted

Confusion
Frustration
Forgetfulness
Incoherence

Deception
Despair
Despondency
Discouragement
Hopelessness
Insomnia
Self-pity
Suicide Thoughts
Suicide Attempts
Withdrawal

Insecurity
Inferiority
Self-pity
Loneliness
Timidity
Shyness
Inadequacy
Ineptness

Addictions
Compulsive
  Behavior
Nicotine
Alcohol
Drugs
Gambling
Food
Sports
Television
Music
Video Games

Escape
Fantasy
Lazy
Daydreaming
Lethargy

Anger
Hatred
Murder
Rage

Self Deception
Self-delusion
Pride

Pride
Ego
Vanity
Haughtiness
Self-importance
Arrogance

Financial
  Patterns
Greed
Poor Spending
Job Failures
Poverty
Stinginess
Cheating
Stealing

Infirmities
Diseases
Anorexia
Bulimia
Asthma
Miscarriage
Barrenness
Cancer
Lung Disease
Diabetes
  etc

Judgment
Blames
Criticalness
Fault Finding
Scorner
Un-teachable

Curses
Blasphemy
Course Jesting
Gossip
Backbiting
Mockery
Belittling Others

Grief
Heartbreak
Loss
Sadness
Sorrow

Greed
Covetousness
Stealing
Kleptomania
Material Lust

Mental Illness
Compulsions
Confusion
Hallucinations
Insanity
Paranoia
Schizophrenia

Retaliation
Hatred
Cruelty
Spite
Destruction
Sadism

Strife
Contention
Bickering
Argumentative
Fighting
Quarreling
Cursing
Mocking

Paranoia
Jealously
Envy
Suspicion
Distrust
Confrontation

Fatigue
Tiredness
Laziness

Unbelief
Doubt
Skepticism

Shame
Condemnation
Guilt
Overweight
Underweight
Self-hate

Sexual
  Immorality
Masturbation
Adultery
Homosexuality
Fantasies

Mocking
Laughing
Ridicule
Sarcasm
Gossip
Belittling Others

Indecision
Procrastination
Compromise
Confusion
Indifference

169

Idolatry	**Sexual (con't)**	**Perfectionism**	**False Religions**
Food	Incest	Vanity	Hinduism
Money	Rape	Ego	Islam
Clothes	Exposure	Frustration	Shintoism
Possessions	Frigidity	Irritability	Confucianism
	Premarital Sex	Intolerance	Black Muslin
	Pornography	Anger	Buddhism
	Molestation		
	Sodomy		

Music	**Mind Idolatry**	**Impatience**	**Victim**
Heavy Metal	Intellectualism	Agitation	Helplessness
Rap	Rationalization	Frustration	Hopelessness
Acid Rock	Pride	Criticism	Mistrust
	Ego	Intolerance	Suspicious

Occult	**Cults**	**Violence**	**Unworthiness**
Antichrist	Jehovah's Witness	Cruelty	Self-Accusation
Auto Projection	Christian Science	Destruction	Self-Condemnation
Astrology	Mormonism	Feuding	Self-Hatred
Automatic Writing	Bahaism	Hate	Shame
Black Magic	Unitarianism	Murder	Regret
Occult Books	Etc.	Retaliation	Remorse
Witchcraft	Also, any lodge	Torture	
Clairvoyance	society or social		
Crystal Ball	agency using the		
Death/Suicide	bible but omitting		
ESP	the blood Atonement		
Horoscopes	of Jesus Christ		
Hypnosis			
Occult Jewelry	**Religious Spirits**		**Unforgiveness Towards Others**
KKK	Ritualism		List individuals
Levitation	Formalism		_____
Mental Telepathy	Doctrinal Error		_____
Ouija Board	Fear of God		_____
Palm Reading	Fear of Hell		_____
Seances'	Religiosity		_____
Sorcery	Denominational Spirits		_____
Spell or Hex Casting			
Spirit Guides			
Tarot Cards	**Trauma**		
Voodoo	Accident		
Water witching	Emotional Abuse		
White Magic	Verbal Abuse		
Yoga	Physical Abuse		
Meditation	Sexual Abuse		
ETC.	Loss		
	Shock		
	Violence		

NOTES
1. The aforementioned demons are just a sampling of what you may discover during a deliverance session. It is a good thing to familiarize yourself with these and other spirits you will encounter. However, never anticipate in advance; always be lead by the Holy Spirit and listen carefully to the person who will be going through deliverance.

2. It is not possible to rank these tormenting spirits from the most devastating to the least devastating. Each individual is different based upon their past experiences and what generational curses have come down their family's bloodline. However, there are five major categories that seem to always appear: Rejection, Unforgiveness, Bitterness, Guilt, and Sexual Immorality. Each of these will have a variety of sub-categories.

Because of their frequency, we will deal specifically with four of these groupings in the following chapters.

Chapter Twenty-Nine

SPIRIT OF REJECTION

Our basic needs are satisfied by love, respect, acceptance and security. The root of rejection hinders us from receiving these benefits.

Rejection is the master plan of the enemy. He uses rejection to try and destroy the Body of Christ; and to steal your opportunity to be used of God. At one time or another, we all have faced some form of rejection. Rejection is a common, yet extremely tormenting spirit. The following information is not necessary to cast out a spirit of rejection but will assist the deliverance team to assess when it entered and the depth of bondage it has on the individual going through the deliverance process.

Too frequently the problem of rejection is seldom recognized or diagnosed as a problem. Mainly because there can be so many demonic spirits associated with rejection that sometimes the root cause is missed

What Causes Rejection?

Rejection in the Womb
Children can experience rejection even when they are in their mothers' womb; because they are spiritual beings and are able to receive their mother's emotional problems.

Any women who became pregnant through rape, incest, or adultery carry unwanted pregnancies, thus passing on to her unborn child the feeling of rejection.

Any circumstances and attitude a pregnant woman feels or experiences towards the unborn child will influence the baby while in the womb. This is especially true if the pregnancy is unwanted or there is sex preference on the part of the mother or father. If the parents express a strong preference for the child to be a boy or girl and the child does not meet that expectation, it can cause rejection.

Rejection During Childhood

A child's security is acquired during the first six years of life. During this time, the child develops his values, his security and his identity. Following is a list of causes of rejection in childhood:

* A lack of attention or care from parents
* Adoption
* Comparison of siblings
* Harsh or outspoken parental criticism
* Parents lack of interest in listening to the child or lack of interest in the child's activities
* Over-protection
* Excessive control or manipulation
* Abandonment
* Material things in place of love
* Broken home or divorce

Rejection During Adolescence

In many cases, a child growing up during his teenager years will experience different types of rejection. The following list provides us with events, attitudes, or behaviors that can cause rejection in a child's life during his teen years.

* Mental, physical or sexual abuse by parents, friends, teachers or peers
* Shaming a child in front of others
* Family poverty
* Controlling parents
* Pushing children beyond their abilities
* Rejection of the opposite sex

Rejection During Adulthood and/or Marriage

* Guilt over: unwanted pregnancy, abortion, inability to have children, etc.
* Death of a partner
* Divorce
* Infidelity by one's partner

* Mental, physical or sexual cruelty
* Shame due to a physical deformity

* Financial disaster
* Inability to communicate effectively

Regardless of what causes rejection, it will affect our relationship with God, our family, our brothers and sisters, and every interpersonal relationship we are involved in.

Some of us perceive God the same way we perceive our parents. Often times people do not feel worthy of getting close to our Heavenly Father because they automatically expect to be rejected, just as they were at home.

It is also true that rejected parents usually produce rejected children.

For those in the deliverance ministry it is imperative to understand that there are numerous behaviors that can accompany the spirit of rejection. Each of these attitudes and behaviors will, however, fit under one of the following three separate symptoms:

1. <u>Symptoms of the Root of Rejection:</u> (Aggressive Reactions)
    Those who feel rejected tend to:
    a. Refuse physical contact. They dislike, or resist, being touched or embraced physically.
    b. Display emotional harshness. Cold, insensitive and selfish. Often use their tongue as a weapon.
    c. Doubt and lack belief. They lose faith in family, friends and people in general and are usually suspicious of others.
    d. Hold thoughts of vengeance.
    e. Swear and use foul language.
    f. Be argumentative.
    g. Be rebellious.

2. <u>Symptoms of Self-Rejection</u>
    This symptom of rejection deals with personal intimacy and self-respect.

Those who feel rejected tend to:
+ Have low self-esteem. Consider themselves insignificant and worthless.
+ Feel inferior, insecure and inadequate.
+ Experience sadness and grief to the extreme and it manifests as a wounded-spirit
+ Experience self-condemnation.
+ Experience anxiety, worry and depression.

3. Symptoms of Fear of Rejection

Individuals who are afraid of being rejected, tend to behave the same in any given situation.
+ They push themselves to succeed as a means of gaining approval.
+ They become perfectionist.
+ They experience interrupted sleep patterns.
+ If they were rejected as a child they may be emotionally immature.

The aforementioned are some of the symptoms you may find associated with the spirit of rejection. Everyone is different, but <u>be assured the spirit of rejection is extremely common and is a significant tormenting spirit used by Satan to destroy one's life.</u>

Chapter Thirty

THE LACK OF FORGIVNESS

Lack of forgiveness is one of the largest problems in the church today. The consequences of that lack of forgiveness are many wounded believers who in turn tend to hurt others. Not forgiving is an open door to the enemy to destroy our spiritual, emotional and physical lives.

It is not only an open door to a spirit of unforgiveness but if we continue in our lack of forgiveness it is an open door to a spirit of bitterness (See Chapter Thirty-One).

What Forgiveness is Not
To forget or ignore grievances and sweep them under the rug, to deny the fact that we have been hurt, to try and let time heal the wounds and offenses, to make excuses, or to say, "I forgive you" without genuinely doing it. None of these constitute forgiveness.

What is Forgiveness?
To forgive means to set free from all debt, anyone who hurts or offends us. It is simply an act of your will and not an emotion.

"And His Master was angry, and delivered him to the torturers until he should pay all that was due him. So My heavenly Father also will do to you if each of you from his heart, does not forgive his brother his trespasses." Matthew 18:34 & 35

Forgiveness is Not an Option but a Command from the Lord

"For if you forgive men their trespasses, your heavenly Father will also forgive you."

Lack of Forgiveness is a Bait for the Enemy
"But whoever causes one of these little ones who believe in Me to sin, it would be better for him a millstone were hung around his neck; and he were drowned in the depth of the sea. Woe to the world because of offenses! For offense must come, but woe to that man by whom the offense comes!"

Jesus said offenses were necessary. The word offense is very significant. It comes from the word "skandalo," which means a trap or bait. In other words, every time someone offends or hurts us, it could be a trap or bait from the enemy to make us bitter and cause us to either miss out on a blessing or keep us from fulfilling our assigned ministry

As believers we need to learn how to block out offenses through love, keeping in mind that love does not rejoice in iniquity. When we are offended, it is not always someone else's fault.

Sometimes it is our own insecurity and immaturity that causes us to become easily offended, and take everything personally. And sometimes it is someone else either intentionally or unintentionally doing or saying something to offend you. In either case we are obligated by the Word of God to forgive.

The Consequences of Not Forgiving
+ It is an act of disobedience to God.
+ The enemy gains advantage in our lives. When we choose not to forgive, we open a door for the enemy to enter our lives and destroy our homes, finances, health, and so on. Many people do not know how to forgive because they have not yet forgiven themselves for the things they did in the past.
+ Our prayers are hindered. Lack of forgiveness cuts off our communication with God, and causes His presence not to flow in us. Jesus exhorts us to leave whatever we are doing and first settle our debts with those who offend us.
+ God will deliver us to the tormentors (demons). Lack of forgiveness is one

of the major attractions for demons.
+ God does not forgive us. If we refuse to forgive those who hurt us, neither will God forgive us.

The lack of forgiveness causes resentment, bitterness and hate.

Lack of Self-Forgiveness (Sample Prayer)

The inability to forgive oneself is an open door for such spirits as guilt, self-condemnation, feelings of worthlessness, and several others. It will also greatly impede your growth and maturity in your Christian walk.

If those you minister to have difficultly forgiving themselves have them pray a prayer like the one below:

Dear Heavenly Father,

I understand that there is nothing to gain by holding myself in unforgiveness and there is everything to gain by releasing myself from unforgiveness and beginning the process of healing. I want to move forward and make a positive difference in the future. I confess, as sin, the ungodly vows to never forgive myself.

Because Jesus died for my sins, I choose to forgive myself—to no longer punish myself and be angry with myself. I forgive myself for letting the hurt control me and for hurting others out of my hurt. I repent of this behavior and my attitude. I ask for your forgiveness and healing. God, help me to never again retain unforgiveness of myself or others.

Thank You for Your love, and Your grace, and Your mercy as I move forward with You.

In Jesus Name, Amen

Chapter Thirty-One

THE ROOT OF BITTERNESS

Bitterness begins with unforgiveness. If we continue not to forgive others it is an open door to the root of bitterness.

The root of bitterness is one of the primary reasons why believers feel miserable, are physically ill and feel separated from God's grace. It can produce wrath, anger, rage, and swearing.

"Looking diligently lest anyone fall short of the grace of God; lest any root of bitterness springing up cause trouble, and by many become defiled." (Hebrews 12:15).

What is the Root of Bitterness?
Bitterness is an anguish of the soul that makes a person sad, discouraged, and desperate. The person feels a sense of hopelessness, and easily becomes a victim of deception. It is a deep sadness and resentment accompanied by hostility and repressed anger. It can have a negative impact on our personality.

Bitterness is resentment that has turned into a poisonous venom that spreads throughout the soul. It can deepen to the point of destroying our relationship with God, and ruin our entire life if it is left unchecked.

Bitterness is easy to see in others, but very difficult to see in ourselves. Therefore, if those ministering deliverance suspect it may be present it is recommended that you cast it out, even if it has not been discussed previously.

The lack of forgiveness is usually the open door for the root of bitterness. And unforgiveness comes from offenses, difficult circumstances caused by others, or when something or someone is taken from you.

What Causes Bitterness?

The root of bitterness usually begins with a lack of forgiveness that continues through the stages of being offended, hurt, resentful, and then becoming angry, desiring revenge, and finally hatred and a seared conscience.

Specific things that cause bitterness include the following:

When someone or something is taken from you.

Every time something important is taken from us, the enemy sends a spirit of bitterness against us. Naomi had a root of bitterness against God because she thought God had taken her husband and three sons from her.

Many Christians have roots of bitterness because they are dissatisfied with God for one reason or another. In deliverance, when addressing a spirit of bitterness, it is wise to point out (remind the devil and the person receiving deliverance) that God is the author of every good and perfect gift; He is not the author of evil.

A person with a spirit of bitterness will live a life blaming others; always focusing on and talking about what was done to them/or what was taken from them.

Another scriptural example is Esau. When he realized his birthright had been stolen, great bitterness overcame him   (Genesis 27:34-40).

When we have to face circumstances we cannot change.
When an individual faces overwhelming circumstances they cannot control, they feel discouraged, desperate, and develop a sense of hopelessness. When they are subject to a problem and cannot see any possible solution, they are in danger of being attacked by a spirit of bitterness.

During these situations the believer needs to meditate on God's promises and the hope we have in Christ. This is also excellent advice for the person who has just been delivered from a spirit of bitterness.

When someone hurts you.
One of the main reasons for bitterness in our lives is the wounds from the past. This takes us full circle and back to the lack of forgiveness of those who offended us. During deliverance of a spirit of bitterness it may be necessary to come against each item in the cycle of emotional pain, which includes:
1. Revenge,
2. Hatred,
3. Offenses,
4. Hurt (deep hurt, wounded spirit, etc.),
5. Resentment,
6. Bitterness, and
7. Anger.

What Are The Signs of the Root of Bitterness?
The two most obvious signs of someone who has a spirit of bitterness are when a person is constantly complaining about circumstances or relationships; and when a person is constantly swearing or angry. Another common sign is that a person with a root of bitterness will isolate themselves for fear of being hurt again.

Consequences of the Root of Bitterness

Bitterness can separate us from Jesus Christ and from our faith.

"Looking carefully lest anyone fall short of the grace of God; lest any root of bitterness springing up cause trouble and by this many become defiled." (Hebrews 12:15)

Many physical diseases, including arthritis, ulcers, cancer, insomnia, migraines and back pain, are caused by bitterness.

Bitterness confines us to a prison.
"For I see that you are poisoned by bitterness and bound by iniquity." (Acts 8:2)

Many believers today feel confined in financial or family prisons. Often this is due to their bitterness. Bitterness makes us forget all the goodness we have received from God and from others. It takes over and blinds us so we can no longer see the good in people. Therefore, bitterness in the extreme causes them to believe they are right all the time and everyone else is wrong. Obviously, this spirit will not only negatively affect the individual but those in the church they attend.

The only answer to a spirit of bitterness is forgiveness followed by deliverance.

Chapter Thirty-Two

SPIRIT OF GUILT

Guilt is a problem today for both the believer and non-believer. Society struggles with guilt due to the consequences of the abundant sin in the world. But it is also a problem in the church today.

Many believers still feel guilt for past sins and have yet to forgive themselves, or fully believe in the work that Jesus accomplished on the cross.

Are we better than Christ? Of course not, but why is it we know He can forgive our sins and we can't?

What is Guilt?
The Greek word *"hupodikos"* means one under judgment, one who is suffering the consequences or punishment for his evil actions. It is an emotional feeling of being in a bad relationship with God.

Guilt is actually the result of the enemy coming into our mind and bringing condemnation for something we did in the past, even after we ask the Lord for forgiveness. To avoid accepting guilt we need to use our most powerful offensive weapon, the Word of God, against these thoughts. For example, speak out loud: *"There is now therefore no condemnation to those who are in Christ Jesus..."* (Rom 8:1).

Guilt is the result of two things in our lives:
* Not forgiving ourselves
* Not appropriating Jesus' redemptive work on the cross.

Characteristics of a Person with a Sense of Guilt
Many of the following characteristics are also the names of evil spirits attached to the spirit of guilt and also need to be addressed during deliverance:

Self-punishment

Many individuals when they sin expect to suffer the consequences of that sin before obtaining forgiveness. They think they have to suffer enough before they seek to be pardoned. I have heard people say; "I have to suffer for this because I deserve it." But we can receive forgiveness immediately. To think one has to suffer before receiving forgiveness insults and denies Jesus' sacrifice on the cross. His redemptive work is enough to cancel the need for us to suffer in order to be forgiven or accepted. Yes. There are consequences for sin, but not self-punishment.

Unworthiness

The enemy sends thoughts like: "Why should God answer my prayers? I am not worthy of God's forgiveness after what I have done or God can never use me now." Ever had those thoughts? It is guilt brought on by the lies of the enemy.

Even though we are not worthy, Christ made us worthy by His grace. We need to approach God's throne, trusting and knowing that we are able to do it by His grace.

"That you may walk worthy of the Lord, fully pleasing Him, being fruitful in every good work and increasing in the knowledge of God." (Colossians 1:10)

"Therefore, brethren, having boldness to enter the Holiest by the Blood of Jesus, by a new and living way which He consecrated for us, through the veil, that is, His flesh, and having a High Priest over the house of God..."
(Heb. 10:19-21).

Compulsive behaviors

Often time's people who suffer from guilt take on compulsive behaviors. They may become addicted to drugs, alcohol, sexual adventures, materialism, and physical exercise, food, shopping or being a workaholic.

These individuals are trying to fulfill a void in their soul or are attempting to distract their mind with something other than guilt.

False humility
Many people have the mistaken belief that the more impoverished they are, the more God will love them. They believe they are not worthy of anything and deprive themselves of material things. It is very difficult for this type of a person to receive God's blessings.

Guilt is the Result of Not Forgiving Ourselves!!!!!!!!!!!

Why do Christians find it difficult to forgive themselves?

1. They believe that forgiveness is based on their deeds; that **God** forgives based on our works; rather than the redemptive work of Christ on the cross.

2. They possess a spirit of disbelief. No one can exercise faith in God if they cannot forgive themselves. Disbelief is a hindrance to forgiveness. Many people want to "feel" something special when forgiven, but forgiveness is only received by faith.

3. They expect to repeat their sin. The person knows that God can forgive, but the reason many are unable to forgive themselves is because they believe they are going to keep repeating the sin, over and over again. However, they must be taught that Christ died for our sins regardless of whether they were committed yesterday or today. He even died for every sin we may commit in the future.

The Consequences of Guilt

1. Guilt drains our energy and makes us physically and mentally ill.

2. Guilt blocks our relationship with God. It is very difficult for someone who struggles with guilt to have an intense relationship with anyone, including God. Is there a sin that God cannot forgive? Blasphemy

against the Holy Spirit is the only unforgiveable sin. The blood of Christ forgives and cleanses every other sin.

Some Biblical examples of believers who sinned and were forgiven are: Peter, who denied Jesus, and Paul who persecuted the church. As a believer you are no different than Peter or Paul.

Chapter Thirty-Three

SIGNS OF THE ZODIAC

The astrological signs of man are of great significance for anyone who has participated in the occult or has been involved in astrology (Horoscopes, etc.) You will often discover that particular problems with body parts are linked to their zodiac sign if they have knowingly or innocently participated in either.

SIGN	BIRTH DATE	BODY PART
Aquarius	1/20 to 2/18	Lower Legs
Pices	2/19 to 3/20	Feet
Aries	3/21 to 4/40	Head
Tautus	4/21 to 5/20	Neck & Shoulders
Gemini	5/21 to 6/21	Arms
Cancer	6/22 to 7/22	Chest, Breast, & Lungs
Leo	7/23 to 8/22	Heart
Virgo	8/23 to 9/22	Intestines & Bowels
Libra	9/23 to 10/22	Kidneys
Scorpio	10/23 to 11/21	Loin (Lower Intestine Female Prob.)
Sagittarius	11/22 to 12/20	Upper Leg (thigh)
Capricorn	12/21 to 1/19	Knees

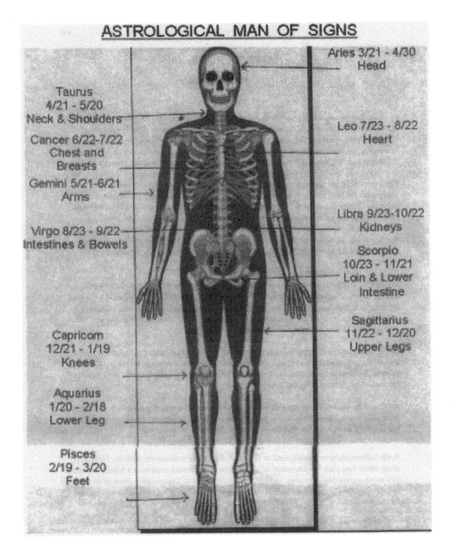

1. Repent of Occult Sin
2. Command Satan to loose you from all occult bondage
3. Break occult curse of sign over your body (be specific)
4. Have deliverance minister command the spirit associated with "your" sign to loose your body.

Chapter Thirty-Four

POLTERGEIST

On more than one occasion I have been asked; "What is a poltergeist? Are haunted houses real? Do evil spirits (often referred to as ghosts) sometimes inhabit houses or other buildings and manifest their presence with ghostly sounds, apparitions, and bizarre happenings? From my personal experience, combined with studying what others have observed and dealt with, I am convinced that they can and do inhabit homes when something evil has given them a legal right.

Poltergeist, from the German word poltern (to knock) and geist (spirit) is the common designation for such spirits. Webster's definition is: "A noisy ghost held to be responsible for mysterious noisy disturbances." Reported manifestations include: the sounds of chains rattling, footsteps, knockings, moans; the sighting of apparitions, lights turning on and off without explanation; the occurrence of the supernatural opening and closing of doors, breaking glass and liquid pouring out from invisible sources; the sensation of cold areas or cold breezes in parts of the house; stuffed animals laughing or crying. Perhaps the most common disturbance is nightmares.

In order for spirits to gain such power to harass and terrorize, there must be some very evil activity or object introduced by either a former or current occupant. Evil activities that provide legal rights to poltergeist can be something as horrendous as murder, suicide or a séance; or as seemingly innocent as a violent or lustful television program allowed to air in the house. Other reasons could be abuse, anger, hatred, bitterness, etc.

Objects that commonly invite the poltergeist spirits are idolatrous images and pictures, witchcraft and occult paraphernalia, including literature from cult organizations (e.g. Mormons, Christian Science, and Jehovah's Witnesses). We actually found a women being harassed and tormented because of a collection of Indian Witchdoctor dolls.

In Deut. 7:26, God's people were warned against bringing idolatrous images into their homes;

"Nor shall you bring an abomination into your house, lest you be doomed to destruction like it; but you shall utterly detest it and utterly abhor it, for it is an accursed thing."

Some individuals have a sentimental or financial attachment to idolatrous artifacts. Perhaps a thing which God calls "an abomination" is a cherished gift from a relative or a friend, or perhaps it is worth a great deal of money. Certain converts to Christ at Ephesus have given us an example to follow:

"Many of those who had practiced magic brought their books together and burned them in the sight of all. And they counted up the value of them, and it totaled fifty thousand pieces of silver." (Acts 19:19)

Remember Achan. He took that which was devoted to God, and it became an accursed thing.

Therefore, the children of Israel could not stand before their enemies. God said, "Neither will I be with you anymore, unless you destroy the accursed thing from among you." (Josh. 7:12)

Any item that invites in a poltergeist spirit must be destroyed.

How does one evict poltergeist spirits?

The procedure is much the same as for one receiving deliverance from indwelling demons or like "cleaning your house" of any demonic presence.

1. Recognize the spiritual authority we have in Christ. We get rid of demons by speaking in faith with the authority in the Name of Jesus.

2. Disassociate oneself from any grounds (known or unknown) that would have given legal right for the spirits to indwell the property. If it is your own sin that gave ground to the devil, sincerely repent and ask for God's forgiveness.

3. Destroy everything that might possibly give any right to the devil. If you

don't know for certain about any given object, honestly and humbly ask for God's will to be revealed.

4. Anoint the house with oil. Be thorough in anointing walls and furnishings.

5. Command every indwelling demon to leave in the name of Jesus.

6. Dedicate the place and all people associated with it to the Lord. Walk through the property and confess that it belongs to the Lord Jesus Christ and that it is a place devoted to Him for the purposes of His Kingdom.

Chapter Thirty-Five

DEMONS CLASSIFIED BY MONTH

Specific demons have been found to be more powerful during certain months of the year. Listed below are twelve demons and the month in which they excel in their power.

This information is referenced in the "Book of Phoenixian Demonology". Phoenician is the extinct Semitic language of the Phoencians.

Each of the following demonic spirits are common to those in the deliverance ministry. But it is of significant importance to understand the powerful influence they can exhibit during a specific month of the year.

January: Belial: A demon of ungodly wickedness, and destruction. Its specific responsibility is to inspire lawlessness and worthlessness.

February: Leviathan: An enormous demon of darkness and chaos; associated with the sea. Leviathan is a transliterated Hebrew word meaning "twisted" or "coiled". The word leviathan in the Hebrew language means a serpent, crocodile or other sea monster. This spirit is a demon principality ruling over other demon principalities. Its specific responsibility is to inspire arrogance and envy.

Other characteristics of leviathan are pride (both spiritual and physical), arrogance, self centeredness, critical attitude, and rebellion.

March: Satan: An angel expelled from heaven and comes from the Hebrew word adversary. It is the personification of evil and all that is hostile to God and the will of God. In the New Testament he is pictured as a dragon or serpent and described as one who has the power of death. He is said to accuse all of mankind before God and opposing the will of God in the world. He is known as the great adversary and his specific responsibility is to inspire mankind to turn away from God.

April: Belphegor: A demon of indifference associated with licentiousness and orgies. He inspires extreme laziness and spiritual apathy. His main role is to sow discord among men and seduce them to evil through the apportionment of wealth.

May: Lucifer: A great angel cast into Hell; also known as the light bringer, the bearer of light and the morning star. Its specific responsibility is to inspire pride and rebellion.

June: Berith: A demon of covenants. It is either a separate god of covenants like Baal or the same demon god of covenants. It is known as the great red harbinger; a kingmaker; and is worshipped by necromancers and alchemists. It inspires megalomania.

July: Beelzebub: Known as the prince of demons and the lord of the flies. Some biblical scholars believe Beelzebub was also known as the "god of filth". This demon inspires gluttony, unholy desire, jealously, war and murder.

August: Astaroth: Is one of the most powerful and respected demons. She was an early goddess among the Sumerians, known as the "Queen of Heaven". She also played a role in the earthly development of other ancient cultures such as the Phoencians, Babylonians, Canaanites, and Egyptians. She is associated with serpents and inspires laziness and vanity.

September: Thammuz: The false god Tammuz is mentioned in Ezekiel 8:14. It is said that it can die and return from the underworld, therefore being a symbol of rebirth and mourning. It inspires torture.

October: Baal: Means Lord and is called the first monarch of Hell. Baal was the principle male god of the Phoenicians and is associated with the power of invisibility and wisdom The specific responsibility of Baal is to inspire idolatry.

November: Asmodai: A demon of wrath. A vicious villain without mercy or compassion. Is known as the prince of demons, and the father of monsters. It specific responsibilities are to inspire gambling, deceit, lust and revenge.

December: Moloch: A demon whose name was probably derived from Melech the king. He was referred to as "the abomination of the children of Ammon" (I Kings 11:7). The primary means of worshipping him was child sacrifice; specifically child sacrifice by parents. Moloch inspires shameful acts, child abuse and abduction.

Chapter Thirty-Six

THE CURSE OF ILLEGITIMACY

The curse of illegitimacy is one example of a generational curse. It is, however, a very common but often overlooked curse in deliverance. Therefore, this chapter is included to both educate and to encourage you to break this curse.

We have already discussed generational curses in some detail, and the curse of illegitimacy is simply another such curse that is passed from one generation to another. However, we have discovered in the past two years just how prevalent this curse is in the body of Christ. And as people pray to break this curse they often begin crying as they experience the release from this heavy burden.

Deuteronomy 23:2-3 says; *"One of illegitimate birth shall not enter the congregation of the Lord; even to the tenth generation none of his descendants shall enter the congregation of the Lord. An Ammonite or Moabite shall not enter the congregation of the Lord; even to the tenth generation none of his descendants shall enter the congregation of the Lord forever. "*

Verse 3 refers to the sin of incest but verse 2 refers to **The Curse of Illegitimacy** or **Curse of the Bastard.**

A bastard curse of illegitimacy effects every child conceived outside of marriage (not just born but conceived). This curse enters a child in the womb at the time of conception and unfortunately brings with it other evil spirits.

Please understand that as we discuss the effects of this curse, it does not mean any one person will have them all; but the person will often demonstrate one or more of these types of behavior and or attitudes.

The child (and adult if the curse isn't broken) will often struggle with such things as shame, guilt, feelings of abandonment, fear, anger, self hatred, feeling invisible, not fitting in, and so forth. In a sense this curse robs them of their identity and they usually feel unloved because they were conceived out of lust rather than love.

The most prominent and noticeable spirits in a person under the curse of illegitimacy are Rejection--Bitterness--Rebellion--and Lust. This person may also have a hard time with intimate relationships; and often struggle with addictions like alcohol, drugs and sexual impurity. Being conceived in lust and not love they often have difficulty both giving or receiving love.

Such a person is usually not content in any one church and may wander from church to church.

Let's look at an example of such a curse in scripture:

II Samuel 11:2-5 says; *"Then it happened one evening that David arose from his bed and walked out on the roof of the king's house. And from the roof he saw a woman bathing, and the woman was very beautiful to behold. So David sent and inquired about the woman. And someone said, 'Is this not Bathsheba, the daughter of Eliam, the wife of Uriah the Hittite?' Then David sent messengers, and took her; and she came to him, and he lay with her, for she was cleansed from her impurity, and she returned to her house. And the woman conceived; so she sent and told David, and said, I am with child."*

David conceived an illegitimate child who brought with it the curse of illegitimacy. The adultery that David committed resulted in a murder to cover up his sexual sin.

The child then died. If this child had lived he would have had to live with this curse; but regardless David's household was also cursed. That is evidenced by his son Solomon who committed the same sin as did his father David.

Based upon this one experience in scripture we can see that adultery, murder, insecurity and sexual sins can arise from and out of the curse of illegitimacy. Therefore, if this curse affects you either directly or from your ancestors (down the bloodline---generational curse) **it must be broken.**

This curse can only be broken with deep-seated repentance beginning with you, your parents and ancestral sins; then asking for God's forgiveness. An example of such a prayer is available at the end of this chapter.

God takes this very seriously, for the curse can go on for 10 generations; which most Bible scholars believe means indefinitely. After breaking the curse of illegitimacy we then must cast out any connected demons and pray for healing of the wounds and damage it may have caused.

This curse of illegitimacy is rampant in the world today and is affecting all races of people. It is destroying the lives of children conceived out of wedlock. God will bring judgment upon those who continue this practice. God will forgive, but you must be ready to break the curse. Jesus is ready and willing to help anyone caught in this curse. He loves you and cares for you.

In the Old Testament the only way to break the curse of illegitimacy was through capital punishment---death to all the family. In the New Testament, Jesus died on the cross to redeem us from the curse of the law---if we repent. His death on the cross substituted the need for us to die in order to break the curse. Praise God! His mercy endures forever and ever.

It is also important to note that an abortion does not set people free from this curse of illegitimacy, even though the child was killed before it had a chance to be born. If you have done this, even though you have asked God to forgive you for the abortion, you still need to repent and remove the curse of illegitimacy through prayer.

If you were conceived out of wedlock; if you conceived a child out of wedlock; if you know that your grandparents or other ancestors conceived a child out of wedlock; you need to pray the following prayer:

Prayer to Break the Curse of Illegitimacy

Heavenly Father, I come to you with a humble heart, asking You in the name of Jesus to forgive me for my involvement in illegitimate children, or the curse upon me as an illegitimate child and I forgive my parents and ancestors.

I repent of my behavior and/or the behavior of my parents and other ancestors for bringing this curse down the bloodline. I know that we cannot change their judgment, but I know from Your Word Father, that Jesus died on Calvary's cross to redeem me from all curses, and right now I ask You Father to redeem me from the curse of illegitimacy. I nail the sins, transgressions and iniquities of myself and my ancestors to the cross, in Jesus name.

Father, break and lift this curse from me, (my spouse) and future generations. I ask You Father, that you restore the blessings in my life, that I can come freely into the congregation of the Lord. Having sweet fellowship with You Father, with Your Son Jesus, the Holy Spirit, and that I can fellowship with my brothers and sisters in Christ.

I thank You Father for Your faithfulness. Help me break any habit patterns that I may have from living under this curse. In the name of Jesus Christ I pray this prayer and thank You for this deliverance. I seal this prayer by the blood of the Lamb.

Chapter Thirty-Seven

THE UNUSUAL AND BIZARRE
Are you kidding me?

The longer one participates in this ministry of deliverance it becomes obvious that the spiritual realm is not only real but represents many answers to the unusual and bizarre phenomenon that exists today. While the list of these supernatural and extraordinary experiences seems almost endless I will mention only a few. This should provide you with sufficient information so that if and when you encounter one of these strange phenomenon's you will understand that it is simply demonic (the expression of an evil spirit).

One of the most common of these strange experiences is called a Poltergeist which was just discussed in the previous chapter. However, the truly unusual and bizarre demonic expressions go far beyond this common experience.

The first such phenomenon is referred to by the medical profession as *Foreign Accent Syndrome* (FAS) which is a rare speech disorder. It is said that the person somehow adopts a vocal speech that sounds like a foreign accent, even though that person has never visited, and has no ancestral relationship, with that particular country.

There are only about 150 cases of this syndrome that have been reported since the early 1940's, although it is suspected that some individuals who experience this phenomenon may not report it.

Both the scientific and medical professions always attempt to come up with a natural cause for any unusual or bizarre experience like the foreign accent syndrome and the other
situations mentioned in this chapter. However, in many cases these explanations are not sufficient to explain these weird and strange experiences..

The only non-spiritual explanation for FAS is damage to the part of the brain that controls rhythm and melody of speech. The causes of this damage is said to be from a stroke, trauma to the brain or possibly MS (Multiple Sclerosis). Others suggest that the damage to the brain affects the coordination of the muscles used when speaking.

The only treatment is speech therapy which attempts to teach you to move your lips differently while speaking. To date there is no reported cases of successful speech therapy for foreign accent syndrome.

The most amazing thing is that many of these cases have been reported from people who have not had any brain damage nor do they have MS. Instead, they had either woke up from a coma, had been under anesthesia, or simply woke up from a night's sleep.

Karen Butler went in for dental surgery and left with numb gums and a foreign accent. Ms. Butler had never been to Europe or any other foreign country, living in America all her life. But after she was put under anesthesia while the dentist removed several teeth, she woke up talking funny. The dentist said, "You will talk normally when the swelling goes down," but she never did. Her accent is now a hodgepodge of English, Irish and a slight mixture of other European accents. She has been diagnosed with foreign accent syndrome with no explanation of how it happened.

Another case was Kath Locket who went to bed one night and woke up with a strange lisp. It continued to worsen over several days until she now has a strong Eastern European accent. She also has been diagnosed with foreign accent syndrome with no explanation as to why this has happened.

A woman in England also woke up with a strong French accent. She also had never visited France nor has any ancestral connection to France, nor has experienced brain damage.

I became interested in this unusual phenomenon when a deliverance minister who works with us called and reported that he had taken an African American woman through deliverance. A woman who had lived in the USA all her life but drifted into a coma during surgery. She woke up from that coma with a Jamaican accent. No stroke, no known brain damage, no MS.

The only explanation that fits these, and other such reported experiences, is the presence of an evil spirit causing a change in their speech pattern. Based upon a variety of case studies it appears that when a person is placed into an unnatural sleep (anesthesia, coma or hypnosis) that person's brain becomes susceptible to demonic attack. In addition, on numerous occasions during deliverance we have experienced demons speaking to us in different voices and accents than the voice and/or accent of the person being delivered.

Another interesting situation we encountered in Mexico while administering deliverance to a woman who only spoke Spanish, although not a case of Foreign Accent Syndrome, was when the woman began speaking to us in English. It was nothing more than the demon we were casting out trying to distract us.

The second unexplained bizarre phenomenon to be discussed is called *The Hat Man* and other *Shadow People*. The Hat Man is a mysterious entity that lurks in the dark. He has been sighted around the world and is ominous and unknown. The Hat Man's wardrobe consists of what can be described as him wearing a long-black trench coat and a flat rimmed gaucho hat. Some have reported seeing a gold watch chain hanging from his side. Facial features have been reported as being a black fog, red eyes or solid black eyes.

Described as a pale, black shadowy, tall and thin with sharp boney fingers and long nails. He may grin, tip his hat, or stare at a person at length. Most sightings never include that he/it speaks.

This figure, called the Hat Man, and other shadow figures, have been described by many as ghosts. But the bible does not ever use the word ghost. But this does not mean there is not an explanation for these shadowy figures in the bible.

People have come to believe that ghosts are actually the departed souls of relatives. They appear as people who have died Hebrews 9:27 says; *"And it is appointed for men to die once, but after this the judgment."* If this is true (and it is) then what are people seeing when they see The Hat Man or other shadow people like figures? The bible sheds some light on this as well.

Revelation 12:7-9; *"And war broke out in heaven: Michael and his angels fought against the dragon; and the dragon and his angels fought. But they did not prevail, nor was there a place found for them in heaven any longer. So the great dragon was cast out, that serpent of old, called the Devil and Satan, who deceives the whole world; he was cast to the earth, and his angels were cast out with him."*

After they were cast from heaven Satan's followers were given a new name: demons. And notice that it says that Satan is a deceiver and leads the whole world astray. Satan is not alone. He is the most powerful but not the only one who does evil. He has helpers. Satan's angels (demons) are his helpers. They are our enemies and they don't know when to give up.

We know that demons (Satan's angels) can appear as men because in Genesis we see angels in the form of men at least twice. During the destruction of Sodom and Gomorrah and when they visited Abraham in the form of man along with God. But this is not all that they can do. They have other forms as well. The phenomenon we are discussing is when they appear as a shadowy figure or the distinct figure known as The Hat Man. Although they appear as shadows, they can move on their own and can pass through solid objects.

Their purpose is unknown. Some of them just stare and others lean over the bed but there is only one report than any of them speak. There is no known reason for their actions except everyone who has seen the hat man or other shadowy figures say there is always a feeling of evil coming from them. Therefore, it is believed that this is simply a scare tactic. Just think how you would feel waking up in the middle of the night seeing a shadowy figure standing over you, or driving down the road and seeing one of more standing in front of you?

I myself have had such an experience. Shortly after our beginning in the deliverance minister I was visited by such a shadowy figure who appeared as the Grim Reaper (spirit of death). He woke me up about 2:00 AM three nights in a row with the intent, I believe, to frighten me in such a way to get me to withdraw from this minister. The first night I was frightened, the next two I just said something like the following: " It's you again, leave in Jesus name." And he did, never to return.

Satan's demons are busy attempting to deceive and scare us, but always remember this: Jesus has authority over them and He has given you authority over them. Just command them to leave in His name. James 4:7, "...submit to God, resist the devil and he will flee from you."

The third phenomenon is truly a deception of the devil. It is called the Kundalini spirit which has invaded the church and in essence is a false Holy Spirit. It comes out of religious cults like Hinduism, Eastern Religions and Kundalini Yoga.

It was brought into America by Rodney Howard Brown in about 1993 when he held meetings all across the country. He called himself the "holy ghost bar tender." He would lay hands on people, or wave his hand over people, imparting the spirit of drunkenness and they would break into uncontrollable laughter, start shaking all over or babbling like a baby.

It was also a part of the Toronto Blessing (and to a smaller extent at the Charismatic Revival in Pensacola Florida) where people were seen acting drunk and falling down, laughing and/or shaking uncontrollably, jerking back and forth, and so on. Some people roared like lions and made other animal noises.

The charismatic movement embraced these actions as a new move of the Holy Spirit and it spread around the world in a very short time. The question that needed to be ask was this: why are the manifestations said to be of the Holy Spirit when they are the same as the manifestations seen in Hinduism, Eastern Religions and the Kundalini cults, especially when they are not found in scripture? There is also no mention of such things in any classic Christianity anywhere.

I had the misfortune of attending one of Rodney Howard Brown's meetings but fortunately my wife and I both had a check in our spirit and refused to let him lay hands on us.

It is said that this kundalini spirit is like a false Holy Spirit and can even perform healing and miracles. We all know that the bible warns us that in the end times there will be seducing spirits, perilous times and lying signs and wonders. It also says we are to be sober and watchful. We see this through all the prophecies of the end times. This is the period we are in now and we are seeing weird signs and wonders, and a movement that promotes drunkenness.

The charismatic movement should have recognized this and rejected it. However, it seems the hunger for a move of God was so great the church was easily influenced by this seducing spirit called kundalini. True revival is represented by souls being saved, people being baptized in the Holy Spirit and delivered from evil spirits like kundalini.

For the most part the frequency of these manifestations have diminished greatly over the years but the church must always remain alert.

For more information on the kundalini spirit go to you tube and watch: <u>Do Not Be Deceived: Kundalini warning Documentary by Andrew Strom.</u>

The last unusual and bizarre experience was the result of evil spirits entering an individual through a blood transfusion and an organ transplant. A woman came to our church for deliverance who reported she had received two organ transplants of both the liver and kidney, as well as several blood transfusions -- I believe the number of transfusions was 16.

During her deliverance we discovered some shocking news. One of the spirits cast out was rejection (see Chapter 29), after which another spirit began to show signs of manifesting. When asked its name, it said "I am the other rejection" (confirming that a person can have more than one spirit of the same name). When asked how it came in, it replied in a man's voice, "I came in from the kidney donor." This woman received an evil spirit of rejection from the man from who she received a kidney.

Side note: Prior to this transplant this young woman never ate sweets but craved them after the transplant. This also indicates that habits and personal tastes can be transferred by organ transplants and/or blood transfusions

During the interview process we discovered that the numerous blood transfusions were required because she had a rare virus called the " B-19 parvovirus." The human parvovirus was discovered in 1974 and was classified as pathogenic. A pathogen is any substance or microorganism that produces detrimental effects on the health of the human body. Almost all viruses are considered pathogenic. <u>The human parvovirus attacks the bones and red blood cells of humans.</u>

This demon also spoke and said, "I consume her blood like Pac man," which is exactly what had been happening. The doctor confirmed that her body contained 100,000 copies of this virus but after deliverance it went steadily down and the last sample reported to us was less than 200 copies of this virus.

Another, even stranger, experience occurred during a recent deliverance we commanded a demon to leave the woman we were ministering to and go to the pit. The demon responded in an unusually garbled voice saying; please send me to the water." Although it is not uncommon for demons to speak to us, this was the first time we had heard such a request.

We learned years ago that many of the most powerful demons we deal with are associated with water and are often referred to as sea creatures. The two most promenade are Leviathan and Rahab. But since this request was never previously expressed we decided to research it further.

The simplest way to explain what was learned is as follows: The torment that demons receive after being cast out is severe since they failed to complete their assigned task. If they are cast into water their torment is less severe because water gives them a form...."they are now in a body of water."

These are just five of the strange and unusual phenomenon's we have encountered during our recent years in the deliverance ministry. Each can be traced back to the activities of demonic spirits.

Other such pheromone that you may want to research are : werewolf syndrome, alien abductions and UFO's, haunted paintings where evil spirits attach themselves to paintings, the music and sexual spirit of pan, and other unusual and bizarre demonic phenomenon. Each of these phenomenon, along with those previous mentioned, have not only been seen but in many cases the associated spirits have been cast out of people who suffered from their torment.

Chapter Thirty-Eight

INCUBUS AND SUCCUBUS

This is not extremely common but if you enter the deliverance ministry it is something that you will encounter occasionally. We have ministered to both men and women who have been sexually attacked by a demon. They experience an invisible, but very real, presence of someone on top of them. You know immediately that it is ungodly and it is a very frightening experience.

Incubus and succubus spirits are familiar spirits that take on female and male identities in order to engage in sex with humans. Incubus spirits take on male identities, and succubus spirits take on female identities. These definitions can be found in the dictionary.

The encounter of these spirits has not been a common occurrence but certainly we have seen it enough times to know how real and tormenting it is to the person these demons attack. I would expect the incidents to escalate due to the increase in pornography and sexual promiscuity. These influences, along with increasing involvement in witchcraft and the occult, are providing opportunities for the incubus and succubus spirits to enter.

Leviticus 20:6 says; *"And the person who turns after mediums and familiar spirits, to prostitute himself with them, I will set My face against that person and cut him off from his people."*

We encountered a woman in El Paso, Texas who had experienced such attacks. She had been a very sexually active individual and was living with her boy-friend. They also had a small child.

Her boyfriend got saved and refused to sleep in the same room with her until she got saved and they got married. This women had a rather aggressive personality and she became very upset. . . actually she became extremely angry. A short time later she was attacked by an incubus spirit. As she resisted it even ripped her night shirt.

The end result, after some counseling, was that she accepted Christ, was delivered and they got married. Praise the Lord!

Many people who have incubus and succubus spirits are also involved in the occult but not all. Sexual abuse and promiscuity are also open doors for these spirits.

Chapter Thirty-Nine

DEMONIC MANIFESTATIONS

When demon spirits are cast out they normally leave through the mouth or nose. Spirits are associated with breathing. Both the Hebrews and Greeks had only one word for spirit or breath.

The Greek word is *pneuma*. The Holy Spirit is also associated with breath. After His resurrection Jesus appeared to His disciples and "He breathed on them, and said to them; *"Receive the Holy Spirit (pneuma)."* (John 20:22)

Two of the old popular hymns were "Breath On Me: Breath of God" and "Holy Spirit, Breath On Me." This gives us the idea that we are to breath in the Holy Spirit and breath out the evil spirits. At times when I pray for someone the Lord will tell me to "breath on them" or to "breath a new breath of life into them". When I do this in response to God, the power of the Holy Spirit inevitably touches them.

When evil spirits depart we normally expect some sort of manifestation through the mouth or nose. The most common is coughing. In addition to coughing the most common demonic manifestations include:

1. Crying
2. Drooling,
3. Screaming
4. Belching
5. Yawning
6. Sighing
7. Exhaling
8. Spitting
9. Roaring
10. Excessive sinus drainage

These various manifestations can vary in intensity from something very mild to something quite dramatic. The degree of manifestation in not an indication of the effectiveness of deliverance. Persons who sigh or yawn out their demons are just as delivered as those who have the more violent manifestations.

While the nose and/or mouth are the normal escape route for demons there are others ways they are released. Evil spirits are creatures of darkness and cannot bear to be brought into the light.

When demons are confronted and pressured through spiritual warfare, they will sometimes demonstrate their particular nature in a variety of ways. This is because when their pressure tactics are exposed they may become excited and frenzied and the manifestations that can come forth are limitless. Following are a few examples:

Satan and his demons are identified with serpents (Luke 10:19 & Rev. 12:9). Therefore, it is not surprising that serpentine manifestations are sometimes witnessed. This will cause a person to stick out his/her tongue or cause it to go in and out rapidly. Also the eyes may take on the characteristics of snake eyes. In one case we had a woman crawl on her stomach until we rebuked that type of manifestation and made her sit in a chair.

Another common manifestation occurs in the hands. The hands become numb or tingle. Demons that manifest themselves in this way are usually demons of lust, suicide, murder, or from evil spirits associated with wrong use of the hands like stealing. Sometimes it helps if the person shakes their hands vigorously.

Arthritic spirits also often manifest themselves in the hands. When the demon of arthritis challenged, regardless of the person's age, sometimes their hands will become stiff and the fingers gnarled and take on the appearance of someone who has had arthritis for several years. Spirits of doubt & unbelief and masturbation also can manifest through the hands.

The spirit of death **can** have a significant, and sometimes frightening manifestation for those who have not yet experienced it, when it is commanded to leave. It can actually appear as if the person has actually died: they may stop breathing, eyes are open rolled back in their head, and their skin color becomes pale like that of a dead person.

Demons may cry out in a loud voice (see Matt. 8:29; Mark 1:23; Luke 4:4; Acts 8:7). We have experienced two rather extreme cases where individuals have manifested in this manner. In each case nearly every demon manifested in this manner and they were extremely loud. Both times we were concerned that our neighbors would come running over, or would call the police, fearing that someone was being hurt.

The spirit of pride may manifest in a variety of ways. They may stand erect, fold their arms in an act of defiance, or they tilt their head back with their nose up in the air. *Pain* is also a very common manifestation. Often time's people will want to postpone their deliverance because they are experiencing pain. During deliverance ministry demons will often cause headaches or bring pain to various parts of the body. Spirits of nervousness and tension may cause pain in the back or neck for example. When this happens the deliverance minister should lay hands on the area of pain and command the demon to release them, and when the demon is cast out the pain is alleviated.

Other manifestations that may be witnessed during deliverance ministries include cramps in the legs and arms, nausea, crying and laughing. Note that laughing is usually a mocking spirit trying to make light of the deliverance or to make you think it is gone and the person is just happy. Don't be fooled: It does not indicate that the person is not serious about his/her deliverance; or that the demon has left, because it is often a diversionary tactic.

There are other manifestations that you may witness, but if you are aware of those mentioned you will not have difficulty with any additional manifestations.

Chapter Forty

SHOULD I BE A DELIVERÆNCE MINISTER?

Today's church suffers from spiritual malnutrition. Therefore, the teaching, of deliverance from a biblical perspective and the training of deliverance ministers is greatly needed. But before you enter this ministry count the cost.

Frequently I am asked how I got into the deliverance ministry. Admittedly, it is not something I desired or sought after. God saved my life through this ministry when he sent me a deliverance ministry team when I was severely depressed and strongly considering suicide. Medical doctors were at a loss because medication no longer was effective. I was a Spirit-filled believer but had never even heard of deliverance.

From that time on God just thrust my wife and I into this ministry. He didn't ask our permission, He just opened the door of opportunity with no way of escape. Since that time we have seen literally hundreds of people set free from demonic torment and healed of various illnesses.

There are several reasons most believers avoid the deliverance ministry. Some of the reasons can be found in the discussion below about the demands placed upon those in this ministry. But there are two other reasons that need to be mentioned first. They are lack of knowledge and fear.

Unfortunately, the majority of the Body of Christ either has a limited knowledge of deliverance or has been incorrectly taught about this ministry. As more and more individuals are set free the message of deliverance has spread, which has been helpful in getting the truth in the hands of Christians.

The message about deliverance, generational curses, and spiritual warfare needs to be shared with those in our churches today. One, so that they can take advantage of this awesome gift God has given His church; and also because there is a need for more deliverance ministry teams. This is the reason I decided to teach classes and write this manual. It is also the reason my wife and I do three and four day workshops on this subject.

The second reason people avoid this ministry is fear of demons and fear of men. Many believers still think that if you leave the devil alone, he will leave you alone. Nothing could be further from the truth. To leave the devil alone is to permit Him to work unchallenged.

There is no reason to fear the devil and his demons because Jesus conquered them. In I John 3:8 we are told that Jesus came for the specific purpose of destroying the works of the devil. In Colossians 2:15 it is shown that through the cross Jesus disarmed principalities and powers, made a public display of them, and completely triumphed over them.

Fear can only be overcome when the believer knows their authority in the name of Jesus and understands that Satan has no real power left, unless we give it to him. The devil is simply a liar, deceiver, trespasser, and thief. In addition, John 16:11 tells us that Jesus has already passed judgment on him. It is now the responsibility of the church to execute that judgment.

Every time we come against a demon with authority, in the name of Jesus and in the power of His shed blood, the demons have no choice but to yield. Believers have no need to fear the devil and his demons as they are stripped of their armor (Luke 11:22). The only thing a Christian has to fear is fear itself.

Satan, a known liar and deceiver, will try and make you think that he is going to retaliate. He will tell you that he will attack your family with sickness, injury or something sinister. But you will trample him under your feet. To bring assurance to the person receiving deliverance we always pray and forbid any retaliation and quote the Word that says; *'nothing shall by any means hurt you."* (Luke 10:19)

I am not a demon chaser who looks for a demon behind every door, under every pew or in everyone I meet. I also have never suggested to anyone that they need deliverance. They know if they need it and we only minister to those who request it, and those whom we become convinced are able to walk in it. However, we should never ignore the devil nor the tormenting spirits assigned to individuals, churches, communities, and nations.

Some ministers have suggested that I just go around looking for demons to cast out and that all I ever think about is the devil. Then they suggest we should keep our minds on Jesus and ignore the evil. I have no problem with keeping our minds on Jesus but I can imagine that the devil delights in hearing someone suggest that we should ignore him and his demons. That thought process is a lie of the devil to keep God's people out of spiritual warfare. Scripture says; *"resist the devil and he will flee,"* it does not say ignore him.

The decision of whether we should all be involved in spiritual warfare is no decision at all. Every Christian needs to be actively involved or suffer the consequences of letting the devil do whatever he desires without being challenged. However, the decision of whether to become directly involved in the deliverance ministry as a member of a team is another decision altogether.

Jesus advised his followers to count the cost of discipleship. To serve the Lord requires personal sacrifice. If one is not willing to pay the price he should never commit himself to being a disciple of Christ. This is especially true in the deliverance ministry because there are many demands on those in this ministry.

For example:

Time: Deliverance is very time-consuming. This is true from the viewpoint of the amount of time you will spend with one individual and from the large number of persons to whom you may minister. The demand for deliverance is increasing and unless some are willing to step up and help, the demand will become overwhelming. Anyone who enters the deliverance ministry will understand why it was said of Jesus; *He entered house, and wanted no one to know it, but He could not be hidden.* (Mark 7:24)

Cost: There will also be a financial cost to those in the deliverance ministry. If nothing else the cost of gas to travel to and from the deliverance location must be considered.

Energy: There are times when the deliverance minister will be involved for long hours, although we try and limit each session to between 2 and 3 hours. There are, however, occasions when we travel to different locations where we have several people needing deliverance. In such cases it is often necessary to minister to several people each day.

Patience: You must be a good listener, especially during the interview process (Personal History Form). Many people needing deliverance have a need to express themselves in greater detail than the deliverance team needs. This not only increases the length of time required but also challenges the patience of those on the ministry team. But, we have also discovered that sometimes, as they seem to ramble, they reveal information that becomes critical to a successful deliverance. In addition, we have seen those who have experienced some actual deliverance while they are confessing certain things. It is important to keep them on track but use discernment as to whether or not what they are sharing is, or will be, helpful.

In addition to the aforementioned demands, the deliverance ministry team must be DEDICATED, and DEVOTED to CHRIST. More specifically, those who decide to become part of a deliverance ministry team must have the following characteristics:

Loving and Wise
Deliverance requires individuals who have a genuine compassion for others... not emotional involvement but rather compassion. The deliverance minister will have many opportunities to demonstrate the true character of his/her love. You must be ready to go the second mile and turn the other check. We have, at times, found it necessary to invite people to stay in our home for them to experience a complete deliverance. This requires love, but it also requires WISDOM.

On one occasion we had a demon try to control things in our home, and we have had those who have attacked us with words of abuse and condemnation. We have also had those who used deliverance as a means of finding a place to live for as long as we would let them. My point here is twofold: (1) use discernment before inviting someone into your home; and (2) love for a person should not be expressed by your yielding to the pressures imposed by demons.

Free From Blame

The deliverance minister must be free from demonic interference before he is qualified to minister to others. Unless he has submitted to needed deliverance for himself he will often find an inward resistance that could hinder his own effectiveness.

Bearing Others Burdens

A deliverance minister will listen to many stories of sinful acts and attitudes. He may even minister to people who are respected leaders in the community or in the church who have never shared their inner conflicts and failures to others. But there are two keys points that he must remember. First, he must always minister in confidentially; and second he must minister in love and understanding ...bearing other's burdens and so fulfilling the law of Christ.

Whatever he hears must not affect his relationship with that person. Early on in our ministry we asked God to allow us to forget the specifics of each and every deliverance. We knew we could not carry their burden indefinitely nor did we want to remember sins that Christ has forgiven. In addition, we never wanted to reflect on the ugliness God cleansed through deliverance.

Willingness to Pray and Fast:

Jesus made it clear that some types of demons are stronger than others. He said; *"this kind can come out by nothing but prayer and fasting..."* (Mark 9:29).

The disciples had failed to deliver a young man from a "dumb spirit. "In essence Jesus attributed their failure to a lack of spiritual dedication. We can also fail for the same reason. Jesus recommended prayer and fasting as the remedy for this spiritual condition.

The concept of fasting is being restored in the church today. Fasting is not a way of bargaining for God's power, but a way of crucifying the flesh so that a person's affection is set upon the things above and not upon the things on this earth. Without prayer and fasting one cannot develop the spiritual resources adequate for every encounter with the enemy.

The Good News of Blessings and Benefits
It is important that the impression here is not that the deliverance ministry is all hardship and sacrifice. There are many blessings and benefits; many occasions for joy. Even the very deliverance session itself is an opportunity to worship and praise God.

The Word of God is often used during deliverance, it is the sword of the Spirit and it is used to thrust into the enemy. In addition there is prayer, both in understanding and in the Spirit… prayers of petition, intercession, thanksgiving and praise. There is rejoicing over Christ's sacrifice and His setting the captive free....what I refer to as the thrill of victory.
Through this ministry I have met some beautiful people in God's family. There are truly many Christians who are seeking the fullness of God and who desire a deeper personal relationship with Him. When all shame and pretense is laid aside, you get to know people in a hurry. It is impossible to put a price tag on the value of friendships gained through contacts opened by the deliverance ministry.

The joy of seeing person after person brought into victory and set free is simply awesome. The most frustrating part of pastoral ministry is counseling. You listen, offer advice and give encouragement but usually there is no real remedy. But, through deliverance you can get to the root of the problems and find answers where in the past there was none. Deliverance can bring a Christian from a life of ruin and defeat to a life of stability and fruitfulness.

One of the greatest blessings received through this ministry is the insight gained into the spiritual realm. It becomes apparent that there is a definite line of demarcation between the realm of light and the realm of darkness.

Spiritual awareness is quickened; strategies of the enemy are more easily discerned and it becomes easier to keep from being drawn into fleshly conflicts with others and to keep the warfare in the heavenlies.

Chapter Forty-One

POTENTIAL PITFALLS

The ministry of deliverance is a God ordained method of setting free those in bondage. But it is not without some potential pitfalls (demonic snares).

<u>Those In Ministry</u>
There are two major snares placed in the path of all those in the deliverance ministry which must be avoided at all cost:

First, and most obvious, is pride. Anyone in this ministry must maintain a close personal relationship with their Creator, knowing that He is the deliverer and we are simply a vessel He uses. This alone can assure you of maintaining a humble attitude and avoiding the entrance of pride. In addition, it is also imperative that whenever you share a testimony of a deliverance and/or healing, always give God the glory and avoid using your name, or the name of the individual vessel God used. This again avoids our becoming puffed up **and prideful. Simply be blessed that God is using you to set the captives free.** And finally, if at any time you become "hurt" or "offended" that someone else is lifted up and recognized, and you are not, then get on your knees and ask God to remove that ugly feeling. Pride is right around the corner.

Second, every deliverance minister must maintain their focus on God and not on demons. I encourage anyone involved in the deliverance ministry to learn all they can about the enemy and his strategies, but not at the expense of reducing the time they spend in the Word and prayer. In fact, your increased study of demonology and your participation in the deliverance process should be an indicator that more time in prayer and God's Word is required, not less time.

In other words, do not rejoice in the fact that you have the authority to cast out demons but rather that you are a chosen vessel. Jesus made this clear to the seventy who were sent out in Luke chapter 10. When they returned they were full of joy because the demons were subject to them in Jesus name. But Jesus replied in verses 19 & 20 when He said; "*Behold, I give you authority to trample on serpents and scorpions (demon spirits) and over all the power of the enemy, and nothing by any means shall hurt you. <u>Nevertheless do not rejoice in this, that the spirits are subject to you, but rather rejoice because your names are written in heaven.</u>*"

<u>Those Receiving Deliverance</u>

There are also several pitfalls (snares of the enemy) for the individual receiving deliverance if they fail to fill the empty space left by vacated demons. Immediately after deliverance the candidate should be instructed on how to maintain their new found freedom (this information is found in Chapter Forty-Three entitled "Maintaining Your Deliverance"). If the individual fails to follow these suggestions, when the enemy attempts to convince them deliverance didn't work, and he will try, they take the chance of re-opening the door for the expelled demons to return. The result of this can bring about the following consequences:

The first thing that usually happens is that they began to lose the faith that was developed during the deliverance session as the evil spirits were expelled. In turn, they either slip back into the life style they lived prior to deliverance or they become dependent upon deliverance for everything that comes along. In either case they usually return for additional deliverance. However, if deliverance becomes too easy to obtain a second time and third time, there is a danger that it could actually hinder their spiritual growth, because they become dependent upon deliverance rather than their relationship with God.

<u>This does not mean that we should turn away desperate people in need of additional deliverance.</u> But if people continually return because they think they "feel something" or have developed a fear that someone has "placed a curse on them," or "have returned to their old pattern of living," they need to be encouraged to strengthen their faith through reading the Word, prayer, worship and listening to anointed teaching. Continual deliverance is not a

substitute for personal growth and self discipline or for a lack of commitment to live a Christian life.

If someone does request deliverance multiple times, or after they have backslid, it would be best if the deliverance minister would meet with that person and find out why they are again requesting deliverance. Discover what is going on in their life and educate them on how to defend themselves, how to build their faith, and how to maintain their deliverance. Then pray with them and be available to encourage them. Once the deliverance ministers knows they are committed, a second deliverance can be scheduled.

Teach them that the Word of God is like an onion. It has multiple layers of meaning, nuances, and benefits like protection, peace, understanding, relationship and spiritual growth. The more they pour into Him (His Word), the more He pours these benefits into us. As a deliverance minister, also remember God called us to set them free, not to keep them free. That is their responsibility.

Therefore, do not take on any quilt for their failure to stand and live a righteous life. Also, these pitfalls (snares of the enemy) are not to be feared, just be aware that they exist.

Chapter Forty-Two

THE DELIVERANCE PROCESS

When you minister to a person in bondage, you will almost always encounter a variety of elements that are involved in keeping that person bound. There are often unresolved hurts, strongholds, legal grounds and unclean spirits that must be dealt with before the person is able to come to complete healing and restoration in that area of their life. An effective deliverance minister requires much more than just casting out demons.

The initial step prior to agreeing to deliverance is:

PRE-QUALIFY YOUR CANDIDATE

This is the process of determining whether the person is ready and prepared to go through deliverance, and then capable of maintaining their new found freedom. This is a vital step that saves a lot of time and helps ensure the success of their deliverance. If you enter into a deliverance and the person is not prepared, you will waste a lot time. And even if the deliverance is successful they will walk out the door and the next day pickup those same spirits all over again.

How do you pre-qualify? Before a person is prepared to receive deliverance, they must meet following requirements:

1. They must be a born-again Christian.
    If they are not it is impossible to remove the legal rights by which the demons are holding onto in their life. Legal ground cannot be removed without the forgiveness of sin, and they cannot receive that forgiveness unless they accept Christ as Lord and Savior. As Jesus said in Matthew 15:26, *"It is not good to take the children's bread, and give to the dogs."*

2. They must be willing to give up anything and everything that is ungodly in their lives.
    If, for example, a person enjoys pornography and is unwilling to give it

up, then it would be nearly impossible to cast it out without it coming right back.

3. <u>They must be willing to communicate about their past openly.</u>
It is important that the deliverance minister is aware of the areas of bondage in their life, and the underlying roots to those bondages. If they choose to hide something, it may keep the deliverance minister from effectively diagnosing the roots of their bondage and dealing with them in a product manner.

4. <u>They must be willing to do whatever is necessary after their deliverance in order to come into and maintain their new found freedom.</u>

This often may require them meditating on certain bible passages on a daily basis. This is vital in tearing down strongholds. For example, if a person suffers from low self-esteem, then it may be beneficial for them to study bible passages which speak about the person whom God has made us into, how much He loves us, and how we are created in His image.

If a person has been viewing God as a cruel and distant taskmaster, they should meditate on scriptures which speak of the loving nature of God, how Jesus loved us while we were still sinners, the parable of the prodigal son (Luke 15), etc. The devil builds strongholds on a regular basis, so we must tear down these strongholds (believed lies) through feeding our minds on God's Word regularly.

It is my belief that every candidate should be serious enough about their relationship with Jesus, that they can set aside a reasonable amount of time daily to spend with Him.

Ministering to those who are not established in the Word can be more time consuming and burdensome. Much of the overall deliverance process involves renewing the mind according to the Word of God, and therefore there needs to be a continual washing of the Word (see Ephesians 5:26-27) on a regular basis.

It is much easier to minister to individuals who are built up spiritually through a continual relationship with Jesus Christ. However, in some cases, having this luxury is not possible, as by the time many desperate individuals come through the doors, there is no time to build themselves up and they need immediate attention.

<u>All deliverance candidates must be ready to forgive those who hurt them, be ready to renounce sin, separate themselves from others who live in sin, and they must have a true desire to be set free.</u>

PRE-DELIVERANCE

There are, of course, different approaches utilized by others in the deliverance ministry. What I am going to share is the process the Lord directed us to use several years ago and it has always been successful. We have also studied the methodology of other well-known legitimate deliverance ministries like "The Children's Bread" and discovered our methodology is extremely similar.

Regardless of one's method, there are three major steps to the ministry of deliverance that must be included if you are to have a successful deliverance. The only exception to this is when time is of the essence due to an emergency situation. The three steps, usually translate into the following major components: Teaching, Interviewing, and Casting out Demons.

Each of the following steps can be done in one session if the candidate is knowledgeable about deliverance or they have traveled long distances to receive deliverance. We find this happens frequently but it requires a willingness by everyone to spend a significant amount of time in that one session. The process of the aforementioned three steps will be presented as being accomplished in two separate sessions.

<u>Step One:</u> After someone contacts you (the deliverance ministry team) requesting deliverance the first session consists of pre-qualifying them, teaching them about deliverance and completing the interview process. Most Christians have a very limited knowledge about deliverance and taking the

time to present the biblical evidence for deliverance is not only necessary but will usually relieve any fears or doubts the candidate may have.

The deliverance minister should have a prepared outline of what needs to be taught. For example: Biblical evidence that a Christian can have a demon; how demons gain access; work and activity of evil spirits; how that person may or may not manifest; generational curses; legal rights and strongholds; soul ties; the use of anointing oil; and so forth.

This step should also include explaining the purpose of the interview process (step two) and sharing the six areas you will be looking for: unforgiveness, generational and spoken curses; soul ties; occult involvement; ungodly beliefs; and unclean spirits (to be cast out).

Before they leave the initial session give them a ""Personal Hindrance Inventory" and tell them to circle anything that may be a stronghold in their life; and instruct them to bring it with them for the deliverance session. The completion of this form will assist you in identifying areas of need and save time during the interview process.

It is also imperative that you inform them that everything that is revealed will remain confidential. I requested a long time ago that God remove my memory of all specifics after deliverance has been completed. I knew I could not carry the burden of so many people indefinitely. God has been faithful to my request. I remember those who receive deliverance but never what they were delivered of.

<u>Step Two:</u> Usually the interview process will also be completed during the second session. There is a "Personal History Work Sheet" at the end of this chapter.

The interview process must be thorough! This means asking some very personal questions sometimes. Therefore, unless they insist, it is better not to have the spouse with them during the interview process or during the deliverance.

I usually ask the candidate to begin by talking about their childhood and then see where it leads. As they share "their story" it will become obvious what questions to ask and you can also begin taking notes: listing things under each of the six categories on the Personal History Work Sheet.

It is important to listen closely to what the person has to say as the spirits will often reveal themselves during these conversations. The Holy Spirit will also reveal these things to you and direct you in what questions to ask.

Before they leave make sure the next appointment has been established. It is always best to have these sessions as close together as possible. By now these indwelling demons know their time is limited and may become agitated and begin to "act up" in an attempt to cancel the deliverance.

Therefore, it is also good to suggest to them that they fast, pray and listen to praise music before coming to the next session.

Step Three: The second session consists of breaking generational and spoken curses, and severing all ungodly soul ties. This process can be done by the deliverance minister or the candidate themselves. The process is as follows:

* Ask the Lord for forgiveness of all your sins
* Ask the Lord for forgiveness of the sins of your ancestors on both sides of their family as far back as necessary.
* Put those sins under the blood of Jesus (your sins and the sins of your ancestors)
* Close all open doors.
* Ask the Lord to lift the curse (from the individual being delivered, his/her family and all future generations. This keeps it from continuing down the bloodline).
* Ask the Lord to sever all ungodly soul ties between the candidate and the other person with whom they committed sin. Name the person in each case if possible.

This is also a good time to have the individual renounce any involvement in the occult and to ask for forgiveness.

THE DELIVERANCE

Note: Always have tissue paper, a waste basket, anointing oil and a glass of water available.

After these steps are complete (explaining deliverance, taking a personal history, breaking generational, severing ungodly soul ties) the deliverance minister should adhere to the following format:

1. Explain how demons may manifest and request that the candidate keep their eyes open during the deliverance process.

2. Explain that they are not to pray but keep their airways open; and only to speak when asked to repeat something or if a demon wants to speak through them.

Pray in Jesus Name!!
Thank you Father for Your presence, faithfulness and mercy towards us. Thank You that you have designated this time for *(name of candidate)* to be set free.

First Prayer:
I bind the strongman in everyone here.
I forbid any retaliation against anyone here or their family, friends, pets or belongings.
I forbid any transference of spirits.

Second Prayer: (If dealing with witchcraft)
I break all blood covenants
I break all dedications
   a. All male children
   b. All female children
   c. All first born
I bind the witches covenant in this area
I destroy in Jesus' name Satan's altar, circle and all implements.
I cut off all transfer spirits

<u>Before Starting:</u> "I place angels of the Lord around you (candidate) and I cover you and everyone here with the Blood of Jesus. I put a blood line between you and us that no demon can cross. I bind your hands with the threefold cord of Ecclesiastes 4:2. [4:12b]

Have the Candidate for Deliverance Repeat This Prayer of Forgiveness

Lord, others have trespassed against me, but in obedience to Your command I now forgive each person who has ever hurt me in any way. As an act of my will I now forgive (name them, both living & dead). Lord I bless each of these individuals; I love them with Your love, and I ask that You forgive them also. And since You have forgiven me, I also forgive myself and accept myself in the name of Jesus Christ. The curse of unforgiveness has no more power in my life. Amen

While it is not necessary, I like to have the candidate pray a prayer of confession, expressing their known authority over Satan and his demons. Following is a sample of such a prayer:

[NKJV: "...because He who is in you is greater than he who is in the world."]

I confess that Jesus in my Lord and Savior; I am under the blood of Jesus and in His name I am stronger than all demons because 1 John 4:4 says; "great is He that is in me, than he who is in the world." I confess that I have sinned and ask You for Your forgiveness, and I receive Your forgiveness right now. [1 John 4:4b]
In Jesus name and by His blood, we know that all here have authority and power over Satan and all demonic spirits. Therefore, when this deliverance is concluded, I will forever more be free from all demonic spirits. In Jesus name, Amen

It is also important that the candidate renounce any and all occult involved, confess it as sin and ask for forgiveness.

Each of these prayers will remove any legal rights the enemy has and he then has to leave when commanded to do so ("*resist the enemy and he shall flee*").

At this point you can start casting out demons. Always be led by the Holy Spirit about where to begin. If the candidate has a stubborn spirit and/or spirits of doubt and unbelief, this is the place to start because these particular spirits can and will slow the rest of the deliverance process.

I have also discovered that spirits like rejection, deep hurts, wounded spirit, etc. are important to remove early in the process. These are usually not the strongest demons and their early removal brings confidence and a sense of peace to the person being delivered. I then usually move to areas like anger, bitterness, and unforgiveness. However, always be led by the Holy Spirit.

It is okay to take breaks between demons or demon groupings if the person needs a break.
Remember this is warfare, it may be spiritual but it can be very tiring.

NOTE! IF A Break is taken, before returning to the deliverance session, reestablish bloodlines and post angels etc.

How To Cast Out Demons

It is just as important to know how to cast demons out as it is to know what to cast out. You never have to holler or raise your voice, demons are not hard of hearing. You also do not ask them politely to leave; the bible says "cast them out." This means it is to be done with authority. All evil spirits know you have authority over them but will resist you if they recognize that you don't know your authority over them.

You simply have to say something like this; "I am here because Jesus Christ of Nazareth has given me the authority to cast you out of *(name person)*. Therefore, in the name of Jesus I command you to leave this body."

If it does not leave immediately have the candidate tell it leave:
"I command you to leave me in Jesus name. I do not want or need you."

You can also have the candidate speak these words on behalf of the demon:
"I the spirit of (name it) give up my right to this body and I am going to leave and go to the pit now." At this point the deliverance minister should continue to command the spirit to leave until it goes.

If the spirit continues to resist make sure that all generational curses in this area are broken. Then continue to command it to leave.

229

Always command them to leave and go to the pit. **Never** suggest that they leave and go seek another body because that could open the door for a transference of that spirit to someone else. I have actually heard deliverance ministers suggest that the demon leave and find another body. That is not a good practice.

Chapter Forty-Three

MAINTAINING YOUR DELIVERANCE

Matthew 13:43-45 makes it clear that if we fail to maintain our deliverance we could end up in a worse state than we were prior to our deliverance.

When the deliverance process is completed those ministering deliverance must provide information to assist that individual maintain their new found freedom. The following information has been developed for this very purpose.

There is no greater experience, outside of your salvation, than getting set free from demonic strongholds. But after your deliverance you must take the responsibility to maintain your freedom. You must take responsibility for your own life, your home and your relationship with God.

Remaining free is a lifelong battle that is extremely rewarding and effective, but definitely takes time and effort to adjust to. It requires a whole new way of thinking, and a parting of your old ways (activities, behaviors & attitudes) that originally opened the door to demons.

Deliverance alone is not a "quick fix" permanent solution if you fail to maintain your freedom. It may be relatively quick, but the permanent solution depends on you, and the choices you make after deliverance. Scripture tells us we are not to love the things of this world, but those of the next. This requires a change in our thinking and behavior. Always remember, there is God and there is Satan. Our activities, thoughts, possessions and attitudes will either be of God or of the devil.

In the following pages we are going to discuss a variety of things regarding maintaining your deliverance. Specifically, we will discuss: things you must know, spiritual house cleaning, examining and changing your attitudes, specific activities you must incorporate into your daily life, warfare prayers, scriptures to study and available resources.

Things You Must Know to Maintain Your Deliverance

After your deliverance, the power the demons once had is now broken, but the devil will present new opportunities of sin to see if he can "win" you back - especially in the area(s) you have previously sinned or struggled. This temptation usually occurs shortly after a successful deliverance, but these attacks are now coming from the outside - not from the inside - which makes it easier to resist.

The devil will try and convince you that nothing has changed and it is "business as usual." It is not and he knows he is fighting an uphill battle but you must keep the door closed.

These demons will continue to attack until they realize that you are sold out for Jesus, solid in your new life and focused on doing what is right in God's sight. Satan's attacks will happen throughout your life, but the hardest, most frequent ones will follow closely behind your deliverance.

You must never forget, and recite often, I Corinthians 10:13; *"No temptation (trial or attack) has overtaken you except such is common to (all) man ; but God is faithful, who will not allow you to be tempted beyond what you are able, but with the temptation will also make a way of escape, that you will be able to bear it."*

If you do succumb to temptation and sin, repent quickly and ask for forgiveness. And if a particular evil spirit should enter at that time of weakness you have the authority to cast it out yourself.

Spiritual House Cleaning

It is imperative that after deliverance you clean you house of any item(s) that are not of God - anything that would be offensive to God if He should see, read or hear them. There is a saying, "we are what we eat" which can be applied to other things that we take into our hearts and minds (music, movies, books, etc). Especially look at the areas of your life where the enemy operated most - these are the areas you will be most sensitive to.

Specific things to look for include:
1. Witchcraft/Occult Materials: Ouija boards, tarot cards, crystal ball, etc.

2. Good Luck Items: rosary, rabbits foot, four leaf clover
   (prayer & faith makes things happen - not luck).

3. Music: rock posters, and all music with ungodly words, content or ideas.

4. Books: yoga, new age, holistic healing/health, meditation, psychic, etc.
   (Healing and peace come from the Lord, not someone's philosophy).

5. Videos: pornography, violent movies (Ask yourself, would God like it? If not, the devil does).

6. Antiques of unknown backgrounds: (Where was it from? Who used it?)

7. Souvenirs of other countries: (They may contain images of idols or symbols of other - current or ancient - gods or religions).

8. Ask the Holy Spirit to show you things that are not pleasing to Him.

9. Bless the home out loud: this helps protect you, and your home - it is a good thing to do this daily. (Example: I bless this home and everything in it in the name of Jesus).

Examine and Change Your Activities

We all know the internet can be a great tool for learning, but there is also a lot of bad content out there in cyberspace. It is important to use the internet in a Godly way or you risk the chance of opening doors to demons.

Consider the content of the television programs, commercials, words, images, ideas and activities that are socially accepted today. Give it the God test: Is it something He would watch or listen to? Also does television distract you from praying, reading the Word of God, and thinking about His desires for your life? If the answer to any of these is yes, you need to re-evaluate what and when you watch on television.

<u>Develop a consistent prayer life</u>: Jesus said to keep watch in prayer, thus preventing us from falling into temptation. One attribute prayer develops is self-control. This virtue will help you resist temptation and stand firm in the commands of God. *"Watch and pray, least you enter into temptation. The spirit is indeed willing, but the flesh is weak."* (Matthew 26:41)

Often times the symptoms of one or more of the ejected demons will reappear in an attempt to make you think deliverance didn't work or didn't last. This is a deceiving tactic of the enemy. All you have to do is not receive it and tell him he is a liar and he has to leave---and he will.

<u>Read and study the Word</u>: This is extremely important because the Word of God fills the void created after deliverance. The Word of God is the anchor of the soul, and no one can remain free of temptation and sin, if time is not spent in reading the Word, studying the Word, and meditating on the Word.

It is a good idea after deliverance to speak Bible verses of deliverance and healing over one's self. *"For the Word of God is living and powerful, and sharper than a two-edged sword, piercing even the division of the soul and spirit, and joints and marrow, and is a discerner of the thoughts and intents of the heart."* (Hebrews 4:12)

<u>Receive the Baptism in the Holy Spirit</u> with the evidence of speaking in tongues if you do you have not already done so. This will also fill the void created by deliverance.

<u>Assemble in the church</u>: Sheep who separate themselves from the flock are the most vulnerable to the enemy's attacks. Gathering will allow you to share and develop friendships among brothers and sisters who can help you grow spiritually.

<u>Put on the armor of God</u>: You put on the armor of God with prayer and a confession of your mouth; and then you **live it.** Put it on daily, one piece at a time. (Ephesians chapter 6)

<u>Resist the devil</u>: God has provided all of us with spiritual weapons, so use

them against the devil. These weapons are the blood, the Word, fasting, and prayer. Do these things and you will remain free.

Pray Daily the Spiritual Warfare Prayer It is important that warfare prayers be spoken out loud. These are specific prayers against Satan and his demons and you want them to hear you. Protect your mind: Your mind is the battlefield and where Satan most often attacks attempting to develop strongholds (ungodly and false thought patterns). Therefore, every thought should be determined as to whether or not it is of God or the enemy. If it is not simply reject it. (see 2 Corinthians 10:5). Rebuke all feelings and thoughts of those things from which you were delivered. If you were delivered from anger, for example, rebuke the feelings and thoughts that would lead you to get angry. If you were delivered from a spirit of infirmity (sickness), rebuke those thoughts/symptoms of sickness. The Bible calls those lying vanities. Rebuke them instead of accepting them. For example, say (out loud); *"In the name of Jesus, I rebuke all feelings of anger and all spirits that are trying to make me angry."*

The enemy will try and confuse you and make you feel and think a certain way, but demons can only make you feel as much as you let them.

Know your authority through Jesus Christ. Remember the devil was defeated at the cross, and he knows it, but you still must come against the enemy each day, exercising your authority. The bottom line is that you win; but to do so you must fight.

The key to ultimate victory is to submit yourself to God, resist the devil, and he will flee (see James 4:7).

Self Imposed Curses, Ungodly Beliefs or Curses Spoken About Others
Scripture warns us that idle words are dangerous and that the *"power of life and death are in the tongues"* e.g. "I am always sick," "David never does anything right," "Ralph, you will never amount to anything," and so forth. If you find yourself saying something like this about yourself or others, or believing it about yourself, you are opening doors. When you say these things rebuke them immediately in the name of Jesus. God did not and does not make us sick, confused, forgetful, angry, prideful, stupid, etc. Rebuke

those statements.

Sample Prayers

Remember, God spoke the earth into existence, He didn't think it into existence. The spoken word has tremendous power. You can have a conversation with God, or speak to God in your mind, but to pray spiritual warfare prayers and have an effect upon the enemy, it must **always** be out loud. It does not have to be loud, but it must be loud enough that you can hear yourself speak.

Upon Waking Up: "I cover myself and my family with the blood of Jesus for our protection. In Jesus name I put on the armor of God - the breastplate of righteousness, the sandals of peace, the shield of faith, the helmet of salvation, and I take up the sword of the Spirit."

Before entering a store, workplace, etc: "I cover myself with the blood of Jesus and I forbid any transference of evil, wicked and demonic spirits in the name of Jesus. I bind the strongman in everyone on this property and in this building in the name of Jesus." You will be amazed at how effective this is and how it will change your experience with other people.

Before speaking with someone (phone or in person) - "I bind the strongman in (their name) the name of Jesus.

Every day, preferably before leaving home, read the "Spiritual Warfare Prayer" out loud!

By Faith Accept God's Word as True

Select the items below from which you received deliverance and **meditate** on the scripture(s) presented under that topic. If there are other specific areas from which you were delivered look up those scriptures and study them. Each time you read them it will re-enforce your deliverance and build your faith.

Rejection:

<u>God made you beautiful</u>. *"I praise You because I am fearfully & wonderfully made."* (Psalm 139:14)

<u>God created you for a special purpose</u>. *"For I know the plans I have for you; declares the Lord. Plans to prosper you and not to harm you, plans to give you hope and a future."* (Jer. 29:11)

<u>God doesn't have favorites</u>. *"For God does not show favoritism."* (Romans 2:11)

<u>God can heal your past</u>: *"He heals the brokenhearted and binds up their wounds."* (Psalm 147:3)

<u>God can use your hurts to help others</u>: *"Therefore, encourage one another and build each other up."* (I Thessalonians 5:11)

Anxiety & Worry

You can be free from worry by meditating on God's Word and casting your cares on Jesus. Find comfort and peace through these scriptures as they promise you hope and a future.

"Therefore, I say to you do not worry about your life, what you will eat or what you will drink, nor about your body, what you will put on. Is not life more than food and the body more than clothing? Look at the birds of the air for they neither sow or reap nor gather into barns; yet your heavenly Father feeds them. Which of you who worry can add one cubit to his stature?" (Matthew 6:25-27)

"But seek first the kingdom of God and His righteousness, and all these things (provisions) will be added to you. Therefore, do not worry about tomorrow, for tomorrow will worry about its own things" (Matthew 6:33-34)

"Trust the Lord with all your hear and lean not unto your own understanding; in all your ways acknowledge Him, and He will make your path straight." (Proverbs 3:5-6)

"Do not be anxious about anything, but in everything, by prayer and petition, with thanksgiving, present your request to God. And the peace of God, which transcends all understanding, will guard your hearts and your minds in Christ Jesus." (Philippians 4:6-7)

"Come to Me all you who labor and are heavy laden, and I will give you rest. Take My yoke upon you and learn from Me, for I am gentle and lowly in heart and you will find rest for your soul. For My yoke is easy and My burden is light." (Matthew 11:28-30)

"Cast your cares on the Lord and He will sustain you; He will never let the righteous fall." (Psalm 55:22)

"Cast all your anxiety on Him because He cares for you." (I Peter 5:7)

"Peace I leave with you; My peace I give you. I do not give to you as the world gives. Do not let your heart be troubled and do not be afraid." (John 14:27)

"Let the peace of God rule in your heart..." (Colossians 3:15)

Bitterness, Unforgiveness, Anger

Bitterness, anger and unforgiveness are hatred, which is actually a <u>lack of love</u>.

It is nearly impossible for someone who is flowing in the love of God to hold onto hateful things inside! Therefore, we need to get grounded in the love of Christ, if you want His love to flow through you! The following scriptures will help with this process.

"And I say to you, ask, and it will be given to you; seek, and you will find; knock and it will be opened to you. For anyone who asks receives, and he who seeks finds, and to him who knocks it will be opened." (Luke 11:9-10)

"Draw near to God, and <u>He will draw near to you</u>...." (James 4:8)
"A new commandment I give to you, That you love one another, as I have loved you, that you also love one another." (John 13:34)

"Greater love hath no man than this, that a man lay down his life for his friends." (John 15:13)

"But it is written, Eye has not seen, nor ear heard, nor have entered into the heart of man, the things which God has prepared for those who love Him." (I Corinthians 2:9)

"Behold what manner of love the Father hath bestowed upon us, that we should be called sons of God...(I John 3:1)
Remember, you are not loved for what you have done...but because of who you are! Even before *you* came to Christ, He loved you so much that He died for you!

"But God showed His great love for us by sending Christ to die for us while we were still sinners." (Romans 5:8)

In this was manifested the love of God toward us, because God sent His only begotten Son into the world, that we might live through Him." (I John 4:9)

Control, Manipulation, Intimidation, Pride

These are all part of the Jezebel spirit and, with the exception of pride, are considered witchcraft.

"Let nothing be done through selfish ambition or conceit, but in lowliness of mind let each esteem others better than himself." (Philippians 3:2)

"God resist the proud, but gives grace to the humble." (James 4:6)

"Humble yourself in the sight of the Lord, and He will lift you up." (James 4:10)

"He must increase, but I must decrease." (John 3:30)

"Blessed are the meek, for they shall inherit the earth." (Matthew 5:5)

"When pride comes, then comes shame; but with the humble is wisdom." (Proverbs 11:2)

"He who does not love does not know God, for God is love." (I John 4:4)

Fears
"For you did not receive the spirit of bondage again to fear, but you received the spirit of adoption by whom we cry out, Abba, Father." ((Romans 8:15)

"Yea, though I walk through the valley of the shadow of death, I will fear no evil for You are with me." (Psalm 23:4)

"The Lord is my light and my salvation, whom shall I fear?" (Psalm 27:1)

"The Lord is on my side, I will not fear..." (Psalm 118:6)

"For God has not given me a spirit of fear, but of power and of love and of a sound mind." (II Timothy 1:7)

"Fear not, for I am with you; Be not dismayed, for I am your God. I will strength you, yes. I will help you. I will uphold you with My righteous right hand." (Isaiah 41:10)

"And do not fear those that can kill the body but cannot kill the soul. But rather fear Him who is able to kill both soul and body." (Matthew 10:28)

"There is no fear in love; but perfect love casts out fear." (I John 4:18)

Shame, Guilt and Condemnation
"There is therefore now no condemnation to those who are in Christ Jesus, who do not walk according to the flesh, but according to the Spirit." (Romans 8:1)

"If we confess our sins, He is faithful and just to forgive us our sins and cleanse us from all unrighteousness." (I John 1:9)
"....if anyone sin, we have an Advocate with the Father, Jesus Christ the righteous." (I John 2:1)

"For all have sinned and fallen short of the glory of God." (Romans 3:23)

"For God did not send His Son into the world to condemn the world, but that the world through Him might be saved." (John 3:17)

"For if our heart condemns us, God is greater than our heart, and knows all things." (I John 3:20)

"The Lord redeems the soul of His servants, and none of those who trust in Him shall be condemned." (Psalm 34:22)

Sexual Immorality and Covetousness

"Therefore, put to death your members which are on the earth: fornication, uncleanness, passion, evil desire, and covetousness which is idolatry." (Colossians 3:5)

"For this is the will of your Father, your sanctification, that you should abstain from sexual immorality." (I Thessalonians 4:3)

"Marriage is honorable among all, and the bed undefiled; but fornicators and adulterers God will judge." (Hebrews 13:4)

"For this you know, that no fornicator, unclean person, nor covetous man, who is an idolater, has any inheritance in the kingdom of Christ and God." (Ephesians 5:5)

"If you love Me, keep My commandments." (John 14:15)

"Now the works of the flesh are evident, which are: adultery, fornication, uncleanness, idolatry, sorcery (witchcraft), hatred, contentions, outbursts of wrath, selfish ambitions, dissentions, heresies, envy, murder, drunkenness, revelries, <u>and the like</u>.....those that practice such things will not inherit the kingdom of God." (Galatians 5:19-21)

"Beloved, I beg you as sojourners (strangers) and pilgrims, abstain from fleshly lusts (desires) which war against the soul." (I Peter 2:11)

Infirmities (Sickness & Disease)

"Surely He has borne our grief's (sickness) and carried our sorrows (pain)." (Isaiah 53:4a)

*"Who Himself bore our sins in His own body on the tree, that we, having dies to sins, might live for righteousness---<u>by whose stripes you **were** healed</u>."*

"He Himself took our infirmities and bore our sicknesses." (Matthew 8:17)

"...if you diligently heed the voice of the Lord your God and do what is right in His sight, give an ear to His commandments and keeps all His statutes, I will put none of the diseases on you that I have brought on the Egyptians. <u>For I am the Lord who heals you.</u>" (Exodus 15:26)

"....serve the Lord your God, and He will bless your bread and your water. And I will take sickness away from you." (Exodus 23:25)

"He sent His Word and healed them, and delivered them from their destructions" (Psalm 107:20)

"O Lord My God. I cried out to You, and You healed me." (Psalm 30:2)
"Bless the Lord, O my soul, and forget not all His benefits; who forgives all your iniquities, <u>Who heals all your diseases</u>." ((Psalm 103:2-3)

"....whatever you ask in prayer believing, you will receive." (Matthew 21:22)

Violence

"Then Jesus said to them, Put your sword in its place, for all who take the sword shall perish by the sword." (Matthew 26:52)

"The Lord tests the righteous, but the wicked and the one who loves violence His soul hates" (Psalm 11:5)

"You have heard it was said, an eye for an eye and a tooth for a tooth. But I tell you not to resist an evil person. But whoever slaps you on the right

cheek, turn the other to him also."   (Matthew 5:38-39)

"For we know Him (God) who said, vengeance is Mine, I will repay says the Lord. The Lord will judge His people. " (Hebrews 10:30)

Murder
"You shall not murder." (Exodus 20:13)

"Beloved do not avenge yourself, but rather give place to wrath; for it is written. 'Vengeance is Mine, I will repay,' says the Lord." (Romans 12:19)

Retaliation
"You shall not take vengeance, nor bear any grudge against the children of your people, but you shall love your neighbor as yourself: I am the Lord." (Leviticus 19:18)

"Do not say, 'I will recompense evil,' Wait for the Lord, and He will serve you." (Proverbs 20:22)

"Repay no evil for evil." (Romans 12:17)

Unworthiness or Feeling "Not Good Enough"
"For you were brought with a price (His blood)...Because you are worthy in Him." (I Corinthians 6:20)

"Being confident of this very thing, that He who has begun a good work in you will complete it until the day of Jesus Christ." (Philippians 1:6)

"For you are His workmanship, created in Christ Jesus for good works..." (Ephesians 2:10)

"But you are a chosen generation, a royal priesthood, a holy nation, His own special people, that you may proclaim the praises of Him who called you out of darkness into His marvelous light." (I Peter 2:9)

You are My witness, says the Lord, and My servant <u>whom I have chosen</u>..." (Isaiah 43:10)

Doubt and Unbelief

"But without faith it is impossible to please Him..." (Hebrews 11:6)

"Let him ask in faith, with no doubting, for he who doubts is like a wave of the sea driven and tossed by the wind." (James 1:6)

"And He said to them; 'why are you troubled? And why do doubts arise in your hearts?" (Like 24:38)

"Assuredly I say to you, if you have faith and <u>do not doubt</u>, you will not only do what was done to this fig tree, but also if you say to this mountain, 'Be removed and cast into the sea,' it will be done." (Matthew 21:21)

For assuredly I say to you, whoever says to this mountain, 'Be removed and cast into the sea,' <u>and does not doubt in his heart,</u> but believes that those things he says will come to pass,<u> he will have whatever he says</u>." (Mark 11:23)

Rebellion

"An evil man seeks only rebellion. Therefore a cruel messenger will be sent against him." (Proverbs 17:11)

"God sets the solitary in families; He brings out those who are bound in prosperity; But the rebellious dwell in a dry land." (Psalm 68:6)

"Therefore, if anyone is in Christ, he is a new creation; old things have passed away; behold <u>all things</u> become new." (II Corinthians 5:17)

Abandonment

"When my father and my mother forsake me, then the Lord will take care of me. (Psalm 27:10)

"And the Lord, He is the one that goes before you. He will be with you, He will not leave you or forsake you; do not feat or be dismayed (terrified)."

(Deuteronomy 31:8)

"Having predestined us to adoption as sons by Jesus Christ to Himself, according to the good pleasure of His will." (Ephesians 1:5)

Special Note: Go to www.spiritualfreedomnetwork.com and watch the video by Pastor Henry Shaffer entitled; "The Importance of Maintaining Your Deliverance.

APPENDIX ONE

TYPES OF OCCULTISM

The following lists will help you identify and clear yourself of any hidden abominations. The rapid increase of demonic manifestations makes it impossible for the list to be exhaustive. Ask the Holy Spirit to reveal to you any specific exposure or involvement you may have forgotten.

* Fortune telling (Prov. 3:5-7)
* Anything that predicts the future or advises your life (Isa. 47:13; II Kings 1:1-4)
* Astrology
* Horoscopes
* Birth signs
* Kabala
* Clairvoyant
* Palm reading
* Crystal balls
* Pendulums used to predict and detect
* ESP
* Eight ball
* Tarot cards and card laying
* Games such as Ouija Boards & Dungeons and Dragons
* Tea leaf reading
* Handwriting analysis* Mental telepathy
* New Age Therapies

Methods of physical or emotional healings in lieu of God's provision through the stripes of Jesus Christ and His death on the cross. (Isa 53:5; 1 Peter 2:24)

* Acupressure
* Holistic medicine
* Sweat lodges

* Iridology
* Magnetic therapies
* Visualization
* American Indian Lore
* Magic practices
* Copper bracelets and the like
* Polarity therapies
* Crystals for various effects on health and well being
* Psychic surgery
* Drum beating
* Seeking information, personal gain, altered consciousness, influence over others, and seeking information, personal gain, altered consciousness, influence over others, and influence over situations for self or others outside the ways and principles of the Heavenly Father. Actually, everything practiced outside of the will of God and in the power of the Holy Spirit (Gal. 3:1; Rev. 21:8).
* All books, literature, music, etc. dealing with occultism
* ESP
* EST
* U.F.O.'s
* Astral projection
* Psycho kinesis
* Auras
* Parapsychology
* Automatic writing
* Good luck objects or apparel (rabbi feet, horse shoe, keepsakes, souvenirs, etc.)
* Dungeons & Dragon s
* Black, white and neutral magic
* Hypnosis
* Burning candles to influence people or situations
* Incantations
* Levitation
* Magic healing
* Chants

* Charms, good luck items, fetishes, amulets, mascots and metals
* Materialization, apparitions, ghosts, poltergeist or boogers
* Mental science
* Channeling
* Necromancy
* Communicating with the dead
* Curses
* Diving
* Spirit guides
* Psychic powers
* Superstition
* Table tipping
* Trance diagnosis
* Voodoo, Hoodoo
* Self-hypnosis
* Witchcraft
* Sorcery
* Yon-yang
* Spells
* False religions, Cults and Teachings (Gal. 11:3-4).

Religions that deny Jesus Christ is the son of God, virgin born, died and rose again, reject the Trinity or says someone is co-equal with the trinity, worship idols and false gods and/or pray to dead saints and /or dead family members. (I Cor. 11:3-4).

* Arthur Ford
* Burning candles as prayer
* Association for Research and Enlightenment
* Christian Science
* Christodeiphianism
* Astral projection
* Eastern religions and teachings such as Zen, Tao, Buddha, Hinduism, Muslimism, Hare Krishna, Transcendental Meditation, I Ching,

Reincarnation, Karma, Yoga, Idols' incense
* Praying to Mary or any saint
* Rosicrucian's
* Ruth Montgomery
* Eastern Star
* Scientology
* Shrine
* Edgar Cayce
* Soul travel
* Spiritual Frontiers Fellowship
* Inner Peace Movement
* Jean Dixon
*Spiritualism
* Jehovah's Witnesses
* Swendenborgianism
* Masonic Lodge
* Mormonism
* New Age Movement
* Unitarians
* New World Order

Other Areas of Occultism

* Some dolls and stuffed animals have been found to cause serious problems for children.
* Movies such as The Exorcist, Poltergeist, Wizard of Oz, Gremlins, Harry Potter, and E.T. (Demonic in that it presents levitation, psychic healing, ESP and reincarnation).
* Some rock and roll music ministers oppression and mind control through its beat and backward masking.
* Subliminal advertising and suggestion
* Television programs such as Fantasy Island, Bewitched, Mr. Wizard, Ninja Turtles and many contemporary cartoons.

* Many video games (many are occultic in theme and demonic in nature).

APPENDIX TWO

DELIVERANCES PRAYERS AND CONFESSIONS

The following pages contain prayers that can be used during deliverance. Some individuals prefer to pray their own prayers and I am all for that. But listen carefully to make sure they are all inclusive. If anything is missed you can add it.

There are other deliverance ministers who have a person read the appropriate prayer(s); and some who prefer to pray it and have the person repeat after them. There is no right or wrong way as long as the person prays the prayer with a sincere heart.

Notice that these prayers are not long or filled with useless verbiage to make them sound good. That is not the purpose. Therefore, these prayers are short and to the point. Neither God nor Satan is impressed with fancy words, just the content of what is said.

Opening Prayer

Lord, I choose to be open and submitted to You today. I ask You to bring healing and deliverance from any wounds and hurts from the past. I trust You to not give me more than I can handle. I can and do trust You to be my protector, my shield, and the revealer of any hurts.

Lord, only You know what lies in darkness, the deepest secrets inside me. I ask that You show me any hurts that You want to heal today.

I give You permission to dig deep for the roots of any hidden memories that are affecting my life. I ask You to take the keys to my heart now, unlock the doors and by-pass any denial or deception that may be blocking my memory, or anything else that has hindered me from receiving deliverance and healing.

Lord, as You bring those things to the surface, I ask that You be there to bring healing and to set me free by the power of the cross, through Your shed blood.

General Confession and Prayer

Lord Jesus, I believe that You are the Son of God. You are the Savior come in the flesh to destroy the works of the devil. You died on the cross for my sins and rose up from the dead. I now confess all my sins, known and unknown, and repent of each one. I ask You to forgive me and cleanse me in Your blood. I do believe the blood cleanses me from all sin. Thank You for redeeming me, cleansing me, and sanctifying me in Your blood. Amen!

Commitment to Christ

Heavenly Father, I am Your child, redeemed by the precious blood of Jesus. You have given me life, and I now give my life to You. My heart's desire is to glorify Your Name. I am an ambassador for Christ and a minister of reconciliation. In Your strength I will love, obey and serve You all the days of my life. Amen!

Forgiveness Prayer

Lord, others have trespassed against me, but in obedience to Your command I now forgive each person who has ever hurt me in any way. As an act of my will I now forgive (name them, both living & dead). Lord, I bless each of these individuals; I love them with Your love, and I ask You to forgive them also. And since You have forgiven me, I also forgive and accept myself in the name of Jesus Christ. The curse of unforgiveness has no more power in my life

Occult Confession Prayer

I confess as sin and seek Your forgiveness for every occult involvement. I confess having sought from Satan the help that should only come from God. I renounce every occult activity; I renounce Satan and all his works. I loose myself from him and I take back all the ground I have ever yielded to him. I choose the blessing and not the curse; I choose life and not death.

Loosing From Witchcraft & Related Powers

In the name of Jesus I now rebuke, break and loose myself, and my family, from any and all evil curses operating through charms, vexes, hexes, spells, omens, jinxes, psychic powers, mind control, witchcraft or sorcery, that have been put upon me through any person, or from any cult or occult source. In Jesus name, I command all such demonic powers to leave me when addressed and told to leave. I am the head and not the tail. I am above and not beneath.

Loosing From Domination Prayer

In the name of the Lord Jesus Christ, I renounce, break, and loose myself from all demonic subjection to my mother, father, my grandparents and any other human being, living or dead, who have dominated and controlled me in any way. I thank You, Lord, for setting me free.

Breaking Curses Confession

In the name of Jesus I confess all the sins of my forefathers, and by the redemptive blood of Jesus, I now break the power of every curse passed down to me through my ancestral line. I confess and repent of each and every sin that I have committed, known and unknown, and accept Christ's forgiveness. He has redeemed me from the curse of the law; I choose the blessing and reject the curse. In Jesus' name I break the power of every curse spoken against me. I cancel the force of every prediction spoken about me, whether intentionally or carelessly, that was not according to God's promised blessing, and I bless those who have cursed me. Father, break and lift every curse from me and stop it from going any further down my bloodline. I command every spirit to leave when told to leave.

Breaking Soul Ties

In the name of the Lord Jesus, I now renounce, break, loose myself from all demonic soul ties through sinful sexual encounters or other ungodly behavior in which two or more of us participated. (Note: Be as specific as possible when breaking soul ties, Name each person or sexual partner and verbally renounce the tie with each one.) I accept God's forgiveness for each one. I break all soul ties with: Animals — formed through inordinate affection for animals; Family members — where there is control and possessiveness; Corrupt and depraved companions who have influenced me in perverse ways; The dead — from prolonged mourning over deceased loved ones; and Church related soul ties where I have been a part of church cliques, idolized a pastor or church leader above Christ, or been controlled by anyone in leadership.

APPENDIX THREE

THE FULL ARMOR OF GOD

Full Armor of God Commentary
Plus
The Military Purpose & Spiritual Application

<u>Commentary</u>

In Ephesians 6:10-12 the Apostle Paul admonishes (warns) us to put on the whole armor of God in order to stand against the forces of hell. It is clear that our warfare is not against physical forces, but against invisible powers, which have clearly defined levels of authority in a real, though invisible, sphere of activity. Paul not only warns us of the clearly defined structure of this invisible realm, he also instructs us to take up the whole armor of God in order to maintain a "battle stance" against this unseen satanic structure. All of the armor is not just passive protection for facing the enemy; it is also to be used offensively against these satanic forces.

Note Paul's final direction: we are to be "praying always with all prayers and supplication in the spirit" (verse 18). Therefore, prayer is not part of the armor but a means by which we engage in the battle itself and the purpose for which we are armed. **To put on the armor of God is to prepare for battle. Prayer is the battle itself, with God's Word being our chief weapon against Satan.**

<u>Read Ephesians 6:10-12</u>
These verses tell us we are to be continually ready for spiritual combat. And that we must recognize that it is our demonic enemies that are behind those things that come against us to harm us.

We learn that this is not just an individual responsibility but it is a corporate responsibility of the entire church (notice the word "brethren" is used here by Paul).

In verse 12......not against flesh and blood: One of the church's greatest demands is to discern the spiritual struggle they are in. If we do not we, as individual believers, and as a corporate body, will "wrestle" with human adversaries instead of prayerfully warring against the individual works of hell behind the scenes.

Read Ephesians 6:13-17

The metaphor used here is based on the armor and battle dress of the first century Roman soldier. It is obvious that this military metaphor is intended to show believers that we are engaged in an active battle right now.

Verses 11-14 are used to suggest and support the following:

1. "To stand against," means to aggressively hold at bay or to stand in front of and oppose the enemy (verse 11).
2. We are to actively engage in one-on-one combat (verse 12).
3. We are to be found standing (victorious) after an active battle (verse 13).
4. We are to stand ready for the next battle (verse 14).

In verse 14-17 we are told that each day we are to consciously put on the spiritual armor that God supplies. And that we are to learn and understand the nature of divine protection.

Protection refers to that which is already accomplished and ready (verse 15).

The wicked one is a direct reference to the personal assault of Satan against believers (verse 16)

PIECES OF ARMOR

BELT OF TRUTH
Practical Military Purpose
This was a very important piece to the Roman Soldier's armor. The soldier would put around his waist a wide belt, which is used as a holder for a lot of equipment. There were several loops to hold different swords, and to hold ropes and his ration sack. When a legion conquered a city, the soldier would empty out his ration sack to make room for gold, jewelry, and other loot he picked up. There were also loops on the belt for darts. The belt was tied in several places to keep it in place, so no matter how the soldier moved, fell down, climbed hills, etc., the belt was always in place with his weapons ready to use. If the belt was not straight, then everything would be out of place. This would reduce his efficiency in battle and may even cost him his life.

Spiritual Warfare Application
Just as the soldier had his waist belt to put on every day to keep his armor together, we must apply the Word of God to our lives on a daily basis or we will not be able to maintain our defenses. The belt was the first thing the soldier put on. Just as this is the first thing the Christian must put on. Much of our weaponry and protection depend on the belt.

If we do not use the Word of God as our belt of truth, we have no foundation on which to base our warfare with the enemy. The belt held things together where they needed to be. The truth of God's Word does the same for us.

BREASTPLATE OF RIGHTEOUSNESS
Practical Military Purpose
The Roman's had the ideas for armor design which provided lightweight combined with the ease of movement and protection from bows. The breastplate was attached to the belt by leather thongs passed through rings on the bottom to keep it solidly attached. It was anchored to the belt, and it was above the belt.
Note: The belt had to be put on first and then the breastplate.

One key area protected by the soldier's breastplate was his heart. While the heart is the key organ responsible for sending blood throughout our circulatory system to keep us alive, our spiritual lives can be deadened if our hearts are not right with God.

Spiritual Warfare Application
When you walk in the righteousness of God, it is a weapon against all those slanderous accusations, and outrageous strategies of the devil. The Bible declares that the heart of a man is prone to be tempted according to Matthew 26:41. We are righteous in God's sight because of Jesus has done for us. Right thinking and doing right are parts of righteousness that we are to protect ourselves with.

FIT YOUR FEET WITH THE PREPARATION OF THE GOSPEL OF PEACE
Practical Military Purpose
Some historians credit footwear as one of the greatest reasons why the Roman Army was so victorious over its enemies. The Roman Soldier was equipped with footwear that had spikes on the soles, which provided them with a strong enough stance and balance that it gave them superior posture in battle on hills and uneven terrain. In martial arts, the stance is the most important move and is what is practiced first. It is from the basic stance that all kicks and punches are launched.

Spiritual Warfare Application
Offensively this piece of the gospel will help you stand with your feet firmly planted on the Word of God and stay there, unmoved by the devils threats and lies. It will protect us when we walk through the rough places and keep us steady in the heat of battle. It will keep our spiritual foes where they belong——at our feet.

SHIELD OF FAITH
Practical Military Purpose
The Romans had a long, rectangular, knees to chin shield which protected them from arrows and spears and which could be knelt behind during an arrow barrage. It was quite a bit heavier and clumsier then the smaller Greek circular shield; but there was a series of exercises, a manual of arms, designed to give the soldier flexibility and strength in the use of the shield. Groups of soldiers who were besieging a town could form close together and hold their shields over their heads to make a huge circle to protect the group from fiery arrows.

Spiritual Warfare Application
In this verse, the Roman shield stands for the faith of the believer in the promises of God. Faith is something that all people possess and utilize every day. Romans 10:17 tells us that faith comes through hearing the Word of God. Knowing the bible and the God of the bible gives you greater faith. Remember it is God that fights with you and that is some awesome protection.

HELMET OF SALVATION
Practical Military Purpose
The Romans had the best helmet of the ancient world. Many other nations used helmets of cloth wrappings, animal hides or bone or hooves, etc. The Roman helmet had a chin strap, visor and came down to cover the back of the neck. Officer's helmets had a ridge on the top on which was mounted a plumage or some sort of brush, depending on the rank.

The parts of the Roman helmet were: a lining of leather, softened for comfort and a good fit; the helmet itself was a bronze cast for the soldier and iron alloy helmets for parade dress. A well designed helmet will protect you from an attack from a variety of angles.

Spiritual Warfare Application
The greatest battlefield is our minds. This is the area the enemy wants to attack the most often. One of the key areas Satan wants to damage is the

assurance of our salvation. The Apostle Paul gave us some good advice in Philippians 4:8 when he said; "Finally, brethren, whatsoever things are true, whatsoever things are honest, whatsoever things are just, whatsoever things are pure; whatsoever things are lovely, whatsoever things are of good report; if there is any virtue, and if there is any praise, THINK ON THESE THINGS.

We must be on guard about what runs through our minds. Satan is very subtle in these areas. He has blinded the world and he will do the same to the unsuspecting or careless Christian. We must have a clear mind to be discerning in all situations. This comes by immersing ourselves in God's Word and prayer.

SWORD OF THE SPIRIT
Practical Military Purpose
The Apostle Paul spoke of one of five different types of Roman swords. This one was a two-edged sword with the end turned upward. It inflicted much more damage than the other swords.
Not only was it intended to kill, but it could also rip the enemy's insides to shreds. It only needed to penetrate two or three inches to mortally wound the enemy. It cut in two directions. This was
seen as a deadly and powerful weapon. In today's world it would be the same as the difference between a standard .32 caliber 6 shot revolver and a 9mm semi-automatic pistol with a15 round magazine. Paul describes the Word of God as an awesome and powerful personal weapon against evil.

Spiritual Wan Application
Our sword of the Spirit is the Word of God. When Jesus was tempted by Satan in the wilderness, Jesus quoted His Father's Word and spoke them with authority. Consequently, each Word was like a sword that penetrated Satan. God has given us the authority of His Word because we are all ambassadors of Christ. God speaks with ultimate authority in the universe. He spoke and the universe came into being. When we speak God's Word according to His will, there is no power in the universe that can withstand it.